BENEATH THE BURNOUT

Understanding Burnout, Honoring Your Capacity, and Building a Life You Don't Need to Escape

Dr. Tashina Reeder

This book was created to educate, empower, and inspire healing, wellness, self-reflection, and personal transformation. It is not intended to diagnose, treat, or replace professional medical, mental health, or therapeutic care. Readers are encouraged to seek licensed professional support when needed.

The author shares personal experiences and reflections as part of a broader message of healing and transformation. Certain names, identifying details, characters, and circumstances may have been changed or fictionalized to protect privacy and confidentiality. With the exception of the author's own account in Chapter 1, the stories that open each chapter are fictional composites created for illustration; any resemblance between those characters and actual persons, living or deceased, is purely coincidental.

Published by Soul Care Publishing

Philadelphia, PA

For resources, speaking engagements, or wellness education, visit: www.soulcareservices.org

ISBN: 979-8-90678-440-7

Printed in the United States of America

Dedication

To the woman who has everything together except herself.

To the woman who kept going even when she was tired.

To the woman who believes she needs to control the narrative.

To the woman who survived but forgot how to live.

To the woman everyone calls "strong," but no one checks on.

To the woman carrying everyone else's burdens while hiding her own.

To the woman who has sacrificed her own well-being while taking care of everyone else.

To the woman leading teams, building businesses, serving her community, caring for her family, or answering a calling that has cost her more than she realized.

To the woman who mistakes exhaustion for purpose, overthinking for preparation, and control for peace.

May these pages remind you that your worth has never been measured by how much you can carry.

This is your permission to exhale, honor your capacity, rest, and be free.

Come to me, all you who are weary and burdened, and I will give you rest.

Take my yoke upon you and learn from me, for I am gentle and

humble in heart, and you will find rest for your souls.

For my yoke is easy and my burden is light.

~ Matthew 11:28–30 (NIV)

Dedication

To the woman who has everything together except herself.

To the woman who kept going even when she was tired.

To the woman who believes she needs to control the narrative.

To the woman who survived but forgot how to live.

To the woman everyone calls "strong," but no one checks on.

To the woman carrying everyone else's burdens while hiding her own.

To the woman who has sacrificed her own well-being while taking care of everyone else.

To the woman leading teams, building businesses, serving her community, caring for her family, or answering a calling that has cost her more than she realized.

To the woman who mistakes exhaustion for purpose, overthinking for preparation, and control for peace.

May these pages remind you that your worth has never been measured by how much you can carry.

This is your permission to exhale, honor your capacity, rest, and be free.

Come to me, all you who are weary and burdened, and I will give you rest.

Take my yoke upon you and learn from me, for I am gentle and

humble in heart, and you will find rest for your souls.

For my yoke is easy and my burden is light.

~ Matthew 11:28–30 (NIV)

Table of Contents

HOW TO USE THIS BOOK

A simple map before you begin

PHASE	S.O.U.L. FRAMEWORK	WHAT IT ASKS OF YOU	CHAPTERS
I: The Wake-Up	S: Speak Your Truth	Name what you've been carrying. Stop editing your own experience.	1–2: Your burnout story. The quiet signs.
II: The Soul Shift	O: Own Your Story	Understand why you keep going. Make the connection between your history and your patterns.	3–8: Why you push. The wound beneath. What your body carries.
III: The Reset	U: Uplift Your Wellness	Begin doing things differently. One boundary. One grounding moment. One choice made from capacity.	9–10: Breaking the cycle. The S.O.U.L. Framework™ in full.
IV: The Rebuild	L: Live in Your Truth	Build the external life that matches your internal transformation. Structure that supports you.	11–13: Reconnect. Redefine success. Build rhythms that hold you.

This book moves through four phases. You do not have to read it in a single sitting, and you do not have to start from a place of being ready. You only have to be honest.

Each chapter ends with a Capacity Check section. These are not optional extras. They are where the transformation happens. Reading without the reflection is like attending a therapy session and never speaking.

Read at the pace your life requires, not the pace that feels most productive. Healing is not a destination. It is a direction. This book is the map.

BEFORE YOU BEGIN

Where Are You Right Now?

Before you turn to Chapter 1, take five minutes with these questions. There are no wrong answers. This is not a test of how burned out you are. It is an invitation to be honest about where you are starting, so this book can meet you there.

For each statement, simply note: Yes, Sometimes, or Not yet.

Statement	**Yes**	**Sometimes**	**Not Yet**
1. I feel tired in a way that rest doesn't seem to fix.			
2. I have a hard time naming what is wrong; I just know something feels off.			
3. I understand my patterns, but I'm not always sure where they came from.			

4. I push past what my body is asking for because there's still too much to do.			
5. My sense of worth is closely tied to how much I produce or accomplish.			
6. I have roles or relationships outside of work that drain me just as much.			
7. I know what I need, but I struggle to consistently give it to myself.			
8. I'm starting to make decisions from my values, but the old patterns still pull.			
9. I'm beginning to question whether my definition of success was ever really mine.			
10. I want to build a life that supports me, not just one that functions.			

What Your Answers Might Tell You

IF MOST OF YOUR "YES" RESPONSES ARE IN...	YOU MAY BE IN...	START HERE
Questions 1–2	Phase I: The Wake-Up. You are still learning to name the experience.	Begin at Chapter 1. Read slowly. The naming matters.

Questions 3–6	Phase II: The Soul Shift. You see the patterns but not yet the roots.	Begin at Chapter 3. The why is waiting for you.
Questions 7–8	Phase III: The Reset. You know what to do; the practice is still forming.	Begin at Chapter 9. One decision, made differently.
Questions 9–10	Phase IV: The Integration and Rebuild. You are building. Your life needs to support who you are becoming.	Begin at Chapter 11. The foundation is already there.

It is okay if your answers are scattered across all four. That is not confusion. That is the complexity of being human and information to further explore.

You do not have to be in one neat place to begin or have all the answers. You just have to begin and be honest.

INTRODUCTION

Working Beneath the Burnout

"Heavy is the head that wears the crown."

We've all heard the saying. But what happens when the crown becomes too heavy to carry?

When does responsibility become resentment?

When does strength become survival?

When does success begin to cost you yourself?

Maybe the question isn't whether you're capable of carrying the crown.

You've proven you can. The better question is the one we don't want to ask.

Is the weight you're carrying still yours to bear?

If any of this hit home, you're not alone. There comes a moment when something feels off. Not wrong enough to stop everything, not dramatic enough to fall apart, just off. You are still showing up, still leading, still responding to emails, still taking care of your responsibilities and the people who depend on you. From the outside, your life may look full, productive, even successful.

But internally, something feels heavier than it should.

You are tired.

Not the kind of tiredness that a nap can fix. Not the kind that disappears after a weekend of rest. This is a deeper fatigue, one that lingers in your body, follows you into your thoughts, and shows up in subtle ways throughout your day. It may look like irritability, difficulty focusing, emotional distance, or a sense that you are moving through your life on autopilot. You are functioning but not fully present. You are accomplishing, but not necessarily feeling connected to what you are doing.

Burnout does not always look like collapse. In many cases, it looks like consistency. It looks like being dependable, responsible, and high-performing while running on empty. It can also show up alongside overwhelm, stress, and anxiety. But let me be clear. Stress itself is not burnout. Stress is a normal part of being human. We all experience seasons when life feels heavy, demanding, or overwhelming. Burnout becomes a concern when those demands remain high for an extended period of time without enough recovery, support, or space to replenish what is being depleted.

The World Health Organization (WHO, 2019) identifies burnout as an occupational phenomenon that results from chronic workplace stress that has not been successfully managed. It is characterized by three dimensions: persistent exhaustion or energy depletion, growing mental distance or cynicism toward one's work, and a reduced sense of professional effectiveness.

While the WHO definition specifically centers the workplace, chronic depletion does not always stay confined to work. Similar patterns can develop when the ongoing demands of caregiving, relationships, leadership, ministry, parenting, and other areas of life continue to exceed what we have available to carry them. Throughout this book, I will look at burnout through that broader lens while remaining clear about how it is formally defined.

That distinction matters because burnout is the warning. Living beyond your capacity is the deeper problem.

For many women, the deeper issue is not simply stress or overwork. It is living beyond their emotional, mental, physical, relational, and spiritual capacity for so long that exhaustion begins to feel normal and survival starts to look like success.

That is why this book is not only about understanding burnout. It is about learning to recognize, respect, and honor your capacity before you have nothing left to give.

Before We Go Any Further...

I'd like to define one word that will become the foundation of everything you read from this point forward. It's a word we use often but rarely stop to examine. That word is capacity.

While burnout has been widely defined and studied, capacity is the central philosophy of this book. I use the word capacity to describe something much deeper than time management, productivity, or simply having enough energy. It becomes the lens through which we will explore burnout, boundaries, relationships, leadership, purpose, and ultimately, the life you're creating.

For this book, I define capacity as:

The emotional, mental, physical, relational, and spiritual space you have available to carry the responsibilities of your life in a healthy, sustainable, and life-giving way.

It is not about how much you can do. It is about what you can carry without losing yourself in the process.

Here is what I have come to believe, both as a clinician and as a woman who has lived this. The problem is rarely that we lack capacity. The problem is that many of us have been living beyond our capacity for so long that exceeding our limits feels normal.

Burnout rarely happens because of one hard week. It happens when what you are carrying consistently exceeds what your mind, body, and spirit were designed to hold, without enough support, recovery, or rest for an extended period of time.

Throughout this book, I'll continually invite you to return to one life-changing question:

Do I truly have the capacity for this?

Not just today. Not just in this season. But in this moment, with everything my life is already asking of me.

The question is not, "Can I do this?" You have proven, over and over, that you can do almost anything. The question that matters is whether you have the capacity to do it well, without abandoning yourself in the process. It will not always be a comfortable question. It may ask you to tell yourself the truth about things you have been avoiding for a long time. But it is the question that leads to freedom, not just relief.

Burnout may have brought you to this book, but I hope wellness is where you'll arrive. Together, we'll explore what it means to honor your capacity, redefine success, and build a life where wellness and ambition can coexist.

When many people hear the word *wellness,* they think about self-care routines, spa days, vacations, or taking occasional breaks. While those practices have value, the kind of wellness we're pursuing in this book reaches much deeper. Wellness is learning to live in a way that honors your emotional, mental, physical, relational, and spiritual capacity. It is choosing a way of living where your well-being is no longer sacrificed in the pursuit of achievement. It is creating a life where success no longer costs you yourself.

Capacity is your internal reserve. Wellness is how you steward it.

An Invitation

Everything that follows is an invitation, not simply to recover from burnout, but to build a life that honors your capacity before burnout ever has the chance to return.

At some point, many of us learned how to keep going regardless of how we felt. We learned to prioritize responsibilities over rest and to measure our value by what we produce. Over time, those patterns create a quiet disconnection from ourselves, so subtle that we often did not recognize it until burnout demanded our attention.

This book is an invitation to pause before saying yes, to reflect before taking on more, and to make decisions that align not only with your goals, but also with your well-being. *Beneath the Burnout* is an invitation to reconnect with yourself, honor what matters most, and create a life shaped by your values rather than constantly driven by obligation.

We are living in a culture where overworking is normalized, productivity is praised, and slowing down feels uncomfortable and even unsafe. It is no surprise that exhaustion begins to feel normal. Wellness is not about doing less, but rather learning to live in a way that honors your capacity.

During the writing of this book, I watched a powerful cultural conversation unfold. Following the 2024 presidential election, many Black women publicly declared they were choosing rest. After decades of showing up, leading, organizing, advocating, caregiving, and carrying the emotional weight of families, communities, and workplaces, many simply said, "I'm tired."

For some, rest became an act of resistance. For others, it became an act of survival.

While the movement emerged within a specific political moment, it reflected something much older, a collective exhaustion rooted in generations of overfunctioning, responsibility, and the expectation that Black women would continue carrying more while asking for less.

Whether or not you identify with that experience, the invitation remains the same: **What have you been carrying that exceeded your capacity long ago?**

Over the years, I have worked with individuals who appear to have everything together on the outside while feeling depleted on the inside. As a trained clinician and trauma-informed practitioner, I have supported many high-achieving women who are capable, responsible, and deeply committed, yet quietly overwhelmed and disconnected from themselves. I am also a woman who has lived this experience.

My own journey has included navigating identity shifts, health challenges, and seasons of grief that required me to rebuild not only my life but my relationship with myself. I understand what it means to be strong for extended periods of time and the cost of sustaining that strength without adequate care. Burnout, for me, was not a single moment. It was a pattern that unfolded over time.

This book is also about balance, but balance does not look the same for everyone. For me, it has meant learning how to find my soul's rhythm beneath the noise of life. That rhythm is not based on perfection or constant productivity, but on alignment, values, faith, and intentional choices. It is about learning how to slow down and permitting myself to move in a way that respects my limits, honors my needs, and allows me to show up fully without abandoning myself in the process.

And I am still learning. This is an ongoing practice, one that continues to evolve as I grow.

What This Book Will Give You

This book will not fix your burnout in a single reading. That is not how healing works, and any book that promises otherwise is asking you to believe something life has already taught you is not true.

What this book will do is give you language for what you have been living. It will help you see the patterns beneath your exhaustion, not just the symptoms on the surface. It will offer you clinical insight without clinical distance, and practical tools without the pretense that tools alone are enough.

Most importantly, this book will invite you to tell yourself the truth about what has been happening and give you a framework for what comes next.

By the time you reach the end of this book, you will have:

- A clear understanding of what burnout actually is, where it comes from, and why it persists even in capable, self-aware people.
- Insight into the specific patterns, beliefs, and conditioning that have kept you in cycles of overextension.
- A framework, the S.O.U.L. Framework™, for moving through burnout in a structured, compassionate, and sustainable way.
- Practical tools for rebuilding your relationship with rest, your identity, your definition of success, and the daily structure of your life.
- Permission, grounded in both research and lived experience, to pursue your ambitions without abandoning yourself in the process.

You do not have to lose your drive to be well. You do not have to choose between ambition and peace. What you have to do is learn to build differently, from the inside out, with your own well-being as part of the foundation rather than the thing you will get to eventually.

Live Within Your Capacity

Many of us were never taught how to live within our capacity. Instead, we have been praised for stretching ourselves beyond our limits, applauded for carrying more than we should, and rewarded for surviving seasons that quietly depleted us.

Somewhere along the way, exhaustion became evidence of commitment. Overextension became proof of love. Busyness became a badge of honor. We learned how to keep going, but not always how to recognize when enough was enough.

The goal is not simply to do less. It is to live differently with greater awareness of what you can carry, what you need, and what it costs you to keep pushing past your limits. The S.O.U.L. Framework™ was created to help you do exactly that.

How This Book Is Organized

The journey ahead follows the same path reflected in this book's subtitle.

First, you'll develop a deeper understanding of burnout: what it is, how it develops, and the many ways it shows up in your life. Next, you'll learn how to recognize and honor your capacity, because sustainable change begins with understanding what you can carry without losing yourself.

Lastly, you'll discover how to build wellness intentionally by creating a life that supports your well-being, protects your peace, and allows your ambition to flourish without constant exhaustion.

Together, these ideas form the foundation of this book and the journey you're about to begin.

To walk that path, the book moves through four phases. Each one builds on the one before it, carrying you from first recognizing what you've been holding to rebuilding a life that can actually hold it. Some phases you'll move through quickly. Others may ask you to slow down and stay a while.

That is not a detour. That is the work.

Phase I: The Wake-Up. Seeing what you have been carrying.

We begin here because nothing changes without awareness. Phase I opens with my own burnout story, told honestly and without the edited version I once offered the world. Chapter 2 then walks you through the quiet signs of burnout, the ones that are easy to dismiss precisely because they do not look like a crisis. By the end of Phase I, you will have language for what has been happening and a clearer picture of what you have been normalizing.

Phase II: The Soul Shift. Understanding what is beneath the burnout.

Burnout is never only about what is on your calendar. Phase II goes deeper, into the patterns, beliefs, and conditioning that keep you pushing past your limits, and into what chronic stress does to your mind and body over time. This is where the clinical foundation of this book lives. Understanding why you move the way you do is what makes it possible to begin moving differently.

Phase III: The Reset. Interrupting the cycle.

Phase III is where change becomes visible. After Phase II helped you understand the patterns beneath your burnout, this phase gives you the tools to interrupt them. It is here that we do the real work of the reset: setting boundaries, protecting your capacity, and moving through the S.O.U.L. Framework™ in full. The framework gives you a structured, repeatable process for working through burnout at any stage, not just now, but whenever life calls you back to this work.

Phase IV: The Integration and Rebuild. Creating a life that supports you.

The final phase is where internal changes start to reshape how your life is built. Phase IV addresses reconnecting with yourself, redefining success on your own terms, and building the systems and rhythms that make healing sustainable over time. This is not the end of the journey. It is where the journey becomes your daily life.

Each phase asks something different of you. All of them ask you to be honest. That is the only prerequisite for this work. Period.

More on How to Use This Book

Each chapter includes a Capacity Check section, and chapters may also offer reflection questions, journaling prompts, and practical applications designed to help you apply what you have read. These are invitations, not assignments. Pause when something resonates. Give yourself space to notice your thoughts, emotions, and physical responses.

While this book draws upon current research, clinical experience, and lived experience, it is not intended to be an exhaustive review of every theory, diagnosis, or variable contributing to burnout.

Burnout is complex and influenced by biological, psychological, relational, occupational, cultural, and societal factors. Rather than attempting to examine every possible cause, this book focuses on the patterns many women experience in everyday life while acknowledging the broader forces that can contribute to chronic stress and burnout.

I will be honest with you. Writing this book felt like writing a second dissertation. Everything in these pages is grounded in my own life experiences, in the experiences women have shared with me, and in what I have witnessed in practice. But we live in a time when a lot of misinformation moves freely through the internet and social media, and it is easy for people to repeat things that were never true to begin with.

So, I made a decision early on. If I state something as fact, I want research to support it. I wanted you to know that what I am sharing has been studied, and that you can go read some of that research for yourself. What you will find in this book is not just my opinion about burnout and capacity. This book is also grounded in evidence, and I am pointing you toward it throughout this book.

Before continuing, it is important to clarify that the stories presented at the beginning of each chapter are fictional, with one exception. Chapter 1 is my own story, told as it happened. The others were intentionally created to provide context, emotional connection, and relatability. The characters are not real individuals, but the experiences, patterns, and emotional truths they represent are very real.

Transformation begins with awareness, and awareness requires slowing down long enough to listen.

Some chapters will land harder than others. Some may bring relief because they finally put words to what you have been carrying. Others may make you uncomfortable because they shine a light on something you have been avoiding. Do not rush past that feeling. Sit with it. It is information, and it may be showing you exactly where your healing needs to begin.

This book can be read alone. It can also be read in community, with a trusted friend, a therapy group, a book club of women who are tired in the same quiet ways. Healing is not meant to happen in isolation. If reading this alongside others creates space for honest conversation, deeper reflection, and meaningful change, that is not a distraction from the work. That is the work.

Finally, if at any point the material surfaces something that feels bigger than a book can hold, please seek support from a licensed mental health professional. This book is a resource. It is not a substitute for clinical care. Knowing when to reach for more is not a sign of weakness. It is an act of courage, self-awareness, and wisdom.

In the next chapter, we begin with a deeper look at what burnout looked like for me, not just as a concept, but as a lived experience. Because before you can change a pattern, you have to recognize it. And if you are here, chances are you have already started to see it for yourself.

PHASE I:
THE WAKE-UP

Seeing What You've Been Carrying

"The same behaviors that kept you safe
are now keeping you tired."

~ Dr. Tashina Reeder

Chapter 1

Nobody Asked Me About My Capacity

My Burnout Story

"Owning our story and loving ourselves
through that process is the bravest thing that we'll ever do."
~ Brené Brown

At first, nothing about my life suggested that I was experiencing burnout. From the outside, I was functioning. Working, showing up, building, supporting others, maintaining the responsibilities that came with both my personal and professional life. I was doing what I had always done: minding my business, handling my affairs, pushing through, and carrying on regardless of how I felt.

There was no dramatic moment. There was no breakdown. Just a slow, gradual shift, subtle enough to ignore at first, but persistent enough that it eventually became impossible to overlook.

My body had already started responding long before my mind was willing to acknowledge it. I told myself I was driven. I was spinning in circles to keep life and business afloat, and I called that ambition. But beneath the hustle was something deeper: a wound that kept me performing for approval I did not need.

There were changes I dismissed. More irritable than usual. Less patient. Easily overwhelmed by things I would have managed without much difficulty. My energy was inconsistent, my focus scattered, my thinking foggy. Sleep no longer felt restorative. Even after resting, I woke up tired.

Burnout does not always arrive as a collapse. It does not just live in your calendar or your to-do list. It hides in the tight smile you wear in meetings while your chest tightens beneath the weight of yet another unspoken expectation to be strong. It settles into your muscles, your breath, and your sleep, whispering through headaches, tense shoulders, and the persistent fatigue you have learned to call normal.

At the time, I questioned whether something was wrong with me physically, emotionally, or mentally. *Was I depressed? Was this a midlife crisis? Was this perimenopause?* What I was experiencing was not a failure to cope. It was a response to prolonged stress.

Burnout and depression share similar symptoms, and for some people, the two overlap. In one study of 1,386 teachers across 18 states, researchers found a strong relationship between the two. Among those identified as burned out, 86% also met criteria for a provisional diagnosis of depression (Schonfeld & Bianchi, 2016).

This overlap has been documented in other high-demand professions as well (Wurm et al., 2016). It is sometimes called functional depression, continuing to perform and meet expectations externally while internally feeling depleted and disconnected. That was my experience. If you recognize yourself in that description, please hear this: you do not have to figure it out alone. A licensed mental health professional can help you understand whether what you are carrying is burnout, depression, or both. Each deserves real care.

I was still functioning. Barely. Still showing up, still meeting responsibilities, but something within me felt increasingly distant and harder to access.

My Home Told the Truth Before I Did

One of the clearest signs was not how I felt. It was what was happening around me. The table where I usually worked slowly disappeared beneath stacks of papers, books, and unfinished projects. Clothes accumulated in my bedroom until it looked like a volcano had erupted across the floor. Even my car became cluttered.

What concerned me was not the mess. It was that I no longer had the motivation to deal with it. I would convince myself I was cleaning, but all I was doing was moving piles from one room to another, shifting clutter from one space into the next without creating order.

It was productivity without progress.

At the time, I thought I had a housekeeping problem. My home was telling the truth about me long before I was ready to tell the truth about myself.

The clutter was only the visible part of what I was carrying. Beneath it, I was also navigating grief and perimenopause, both of which added another layer to my exhaustion. In my experience, hormonal changes affected my mood, energy, sleep, and cognition, and those shifts sometimes mirrored or intensified what burnout already felt like. But because I had spent years pushing through discomfort, I did not recognize those changes as a reason to slow down. I responded as I always had: I kept going at the same pace.

I had learned how to be strong. I had learned how to perform, produce, and meet expectations, even when I was tired. What I had not learned was how to recognize my capacity.

There is nothing inherently wrong with pushing through. Sometimes life requires us to gather what energy we have and keep going through a difficult season, a hard day, or a responsibility that simply has to be handled. The problem is when pushing through stops being something you do when necessary and becomes your normal way of functioning.

That is what happened to me. I pushed through when I was tired. I pushed through when I needed to slow down. I pushed through when my own needs required my attention because there was always something else that felt more urgent, more important, or simply had to get done.

After years of operating from a place of resilience and pushing through, I no longer knew how to stop. Slowing down did not feel natural. It felt like falling behind. And that discomfort kept me moving long after my body had begun asking for something different.

Pushing through had helped me survive difficult seasons. But when it became a chronic way of functioning at the expense of my well-being, it was no longer helping me. It was costing me more than I realized or wanted to admit.

The Wound Beneath the Work

There was a deeper layer I had not fully confronted.

Beneath all the striving was the young college student I had once been, still carrying the sting of being told by a white male professor that I was not "graduate school material."

It was not that I lacked the desire. I wanted to go. But his words did more than question my abilities. They wounded my confidence. My stammering tongue and rapid speech became sources of quiet shame, convincing me that my thoughts did not land as powerfully outside of me as they sounded in my mind.

Somewhere in that conversation, I decided he must be right. I began to believe that I simply was not smart enough. Despite everything I later accomplished, that younger version of me still craved validation and carried a belief I had never fully examined. I held on to it far longer than I realized.

I did not challenge him out loud. I challenged him quietly for years, one degree at a time. Sometimes, I wonder whether he is still alive. If he is, I would love five minutes with him. I would introduce myself as Dr. Reeder, slowly, and then say, "How you like me now?" just to make sure he caught every syllable.

That would be my little clapback. But beneath the humor is a harder truth: for years, I built parts of my identity around proving him wrong. What looked like ambition on the outside was also a wound that kept pushing me to achieve.

My drive was not always rooted in alignment. In some ways, it was rooted in survival.

Even with undeniable evidence of my success, an unspoken belief remained: *You are not enough.* So, I worked harder. Achieved more. Overachieved until excellence became my armor and exhaustion became my normal. I told myself that slowing down would make me unworthy, when in truth, I was chasing worth that had always been mine.

Achievement became a way to secure validation, to create stability, to reinforce my identity. Over time, that pattern became so normalized that I did not question it. I saw it as ambition. I saw it as discipline. I saw it as who I was.

But there is a difference between being driven by purpose and being driven by pressure.

I Am Not the Only One

High-achieving women everywhere are carrying this same silent weight, dressed up as ambition, praised as resilience, and quietly costing them their well-being. We have mastered functioning under pressure so well that burnout hides in plain sight, speaking through our bodies long before our minds are willing to listen.

We are constantly in motion, wearing all the hats. Mother. Wife. Partner. Caretaker. Advocate. Somebody's auntie or grandmother. Most of the women I meet are just like me: brilliant entrepreneurs, top-performing executives, committed leaders. And utterly exhausted.

Bone tired.

Our conversations often begin and end the same way:

"Whew. Gurl, I'm tired, but I gotta get this stuff done."

"I have so much going on. I need a vacation."

"I need a nap, but I don't have time."

"It's a lot."

"I can't. It's gonna be the way it's gonna be."

"I'm over it. Why can't things go as planned?"

"I don't have any help, but I have to do what I have to do."

"I could complain, but I'm not."

It is a shared language of strength and strain. But notice what is missing from every one of those sentences.

Not one of them mentions capacity.

Nobody asked me about mine, either. And I never thought to ask myself. We name what still has to get done. We rarely stop to name how much of ourselves we have left to give.

At the same time, I was watching Black women begin to name that same exhaustion out loud and choosing rest without apologizing for it. Watching that shift became a mirror. I began to see how I had been hustling to fill an invisible void, how my worth had become chained to my output, and how I was still trying to prove myself in rooms that did not always see me.

Survival Mode Has a Salary

During this time, I was building my practice while also working a nine-to-five remotely. On paper, it did not appear overwhelming. I was home, my workload was manageable, and I had the flexibility many people desire.

But the stress had little to do with busyness. It was rooted in the pressure to remain relevant in a toxic work culture. I was constantly generating ideas and developing programming that led to dead ends due to limited financial support and organizational constraints. There were moments I felt like I was existing in the role rather than contributing to it.

Everyone operated in silos. Trust was in short supply. Being asked to complete a task started to feel like being dropped into the Hunger Games. I was always in defense mode, and constantly defending myself was exhausting.

I knew internally that I had outgrown that space. I had conversations with friends about wanting to leave, about feeling ready for something different. But part of me was afraid to let go. The stability of a consistent paycheck felt safe, even when the environment no longer fit. Honestly, I didn't want to start over looking for a new job. I knew I didn't want to work for another organization either. But I wasn't sure if I was finally ready to explore full-time entrepreneurship. I wasn't clear on what I wanted to do. So, I stayed, and in staying, I created additional pressure for myself. I worked harder to prove my relevance, to justify my position, to make something work that no longer fit.

Then, unexpectedly, I was laid off.

Although I had considered leaving, the decision being made for me created a different kind of stress. My response was not relief. It was panic. I began scrambling, developing programs, generating ideas, working longer hours to replace what I had lost.

Instead of slowing down, I accelerated. Instead of resting, I pushed harder. I had been working in survival mode for years, saying yes when I had no capacity, overdelivering even when I was undervalued. And still, it did not protect me.

The truth is, I was already exhausted before the layoff.

The loss of income did not create the burnout. It exposed it.

What felt like a disruption became a necessary interruption. Being laid off forced me to sit still in a way I wasn't used to.

Chasing Clarity Instead of Building It

Part of my burnout was also shaped by my life as a businesswoman. Trying to grow and scale something meaningful, I invested in courses, coaching, mentorship, trainings, anything that promised to get me clear faster. At this point, I probably own enough courses to be a certified expert in Information Collection.

I wasn't lacking information. I was drowning in it.

What I actually had was a hard drive full of modules I never finished and a growing sense that I was chasing clarity instead of building it. Without structure or focus, my attention stayed divided, and that divided attention became its own kind of exhaustion.

Sometimes burnout does not come from doing too much. It comes from doing too many things that do not fit who you are or where you are actually trying to go. Looking back, part of my confusion was that I was out of alignment. I was trying to find clarity while continuing to move in directions that did not fully fit with who I was becoming or what I actually wanted.

Doing everything at once is not the same as doing what is necessary. Giving myself permission to move with intention, to focus on one thing at a time, and to release comparison reduced a lot of the pressure feeding my burnout. That is a practice I am still learning, one course and one boundary at a time.

Functioning Is Not the Same as Well-Being

Burnout did not arrive all at once. It developed through repeated patterns of overextension, emotional suppression, and delayed rest. I felt disconnected from things that once brought me joy. Tasks that were once manageable began to feel heavy. Even in stillness, my mind kept cycling through responsibilities. I was present, but not fully there.

What made this challenging was that nothing about me looked broken. I was meeting expectations. From the outside, I appeared consistent and reliable. That made it easy to minimize what I was feeling and keep operating as if everything was fine.

But my body was telling a different story. I could sit down and fall asleep. I could fall asleep almost anywhere. You could be banging drums around me, and somehow, I could still sleep through it. There were times when I would feel myself getting sleepy while trying to work, and instead of allowing myself to rest, I would shake it off and keep going. I kept pushing myself to finish one more thing when what my body was clearly asking for was sleep.

I was functioning, but I was functioning in the way I had become accustomed to: overriding what I needed in order to keep getting things done. I was not taking care of myself. I was treating exhaustion as something to push through instead of something that deserved my attention.

Eventually, I could no longer continue at the same pace without paying a price. My body began to demand what I had been delaying: rest, attention, and a different way of relating to myself. This was not a moment of failure. It was a moment of awareness.

Slowing down required me to challenge long-held beliefs about productivity, worth, and responsibility. It required me to acknowledge that constantly relying on strength without honoring my limits would eventually lead to exhaustion. Burnout is about carrying too much for too long without support, without space to recover, and without honoring your capacity. Recognizing when we have reached our capacity is not weakness. It is wisdom.

My experience was not isolated. In my work as a clinician, I had seen these patterns in many of the women I supported: high-achieving, capable people managing multiple roles and maintaining appearances while feeling overwhelmed and exhausted. For high-achieving women, and especially for Black women, burnout is often mistaken for resilience because we have become so skilled at functioning while depleted.

Burnout can happen to anyone, but for those of us who handle stress well, it can be harder to recognize. We keep carrying more because we can, until eventually, we cannot. That realization moved me away from self-judgment and toward curiosity. Instead of asking, *What is wrong with me?* I began asking, *How much had I been carrying simply because I had convinced myself that I could?*

Around this time, I also started scheduling two-hour massages every month. They were amazing. Massage is a real form of self-care, and part of it was simply that. But it was also more than that. I carry my stress in my neck and shoulders, sometimes to the point of neck spasms, and the massages became a way of releasing what I did not yet know how to release on my own. It was not that I could not feel the stress. I could. I just had not learned how to ease it myself. Over time, the tightening in my shoulders became a signal I learned to listen for. When I felt it, I knew it was time to slow down, stretch, check in with myself, and reassess what was actually going on.

Grieving What I Chose to Release

This season asked me to grieve two things at once. My relationships, and my own definition of success. Both had to be looked at honestly, and both were harder to release than I expected. I could not keep calling it healing while pouring energy into people and situations that left me depleted.

So, I began paying attention to how I felt after a phone call, a visit, or agreeing to help when I did not have the capacity. Did I feel supported, or was I simply needed? Which relationships lacked reciprocity, and how long had I been pretending not to notice?

That same honesty eventually spilled over into my business.

I was not only holding on to relationships that had run their course. I was also holding on to a brand I had poured myself into. Manifesting HER was my first baby. It was where this work began, the thing that started me building services and programming for women.

But as I grew, the focus of my work kept shifting toward soul care, and I already had a practice named Soul Care Services. Over time, it made more sense to build one consistent brand instead of two. Soul Care Services. Soul Care Academy. That meant letting Manifesting HER step back from center, maybe living on as a course rather than the name everything ran under.

Letting it go was its own kind of grief. Not because it had failed, but because it had done exactly what it was supposed to do. It carried me to the place where I could build what came next. The harder I tried to force those old pieces into a new vision, the more frustrated and unclear I became.

Sometimes we convince ourselves that persistence is faithfulness, when in reality it is resistance.

The business had grown. More importantly, I had grown. The version of me that created it was not the same woman now being called to lead it. That kind of honesty asks you to look at people you love, dreams you once believed in, and identities that once served you, and admit that not everything is meant to come with you into your next season.

What I did not expect was that this would uncover another layer of grief. I knew grief could accompany the loss of any meaningful attachment. But knowing that intellectually and living through the quiet ache of releasing people who are still alive are two very different experiences.

Healing from burnout required me to grieve things I had never named as losses: friendships that ran their course, roles I had outgrown, business ideas that no longer aligned, and relationships that existed more out of history than connection.

There is no memorial service for the version of yourself you lovingly outgrow. No one sends flowers when you finally close the door on a dream that once defined you. But making room for grief also made room for growth. New boundaries. New clarity. And eventually, I began building a business and relationships that reflected who I was becoming rather than requiring me to remain who I had been.

What I Was Calling Normal

For a long time, I believed burnout would look obvious. Something I would recognize immediately, something that would force me to stop in a way I could not ignore.

That was not my experience. The signs were there long before I had language for them. They showed up in my body, my thoughts, my emotions, and the way I moved through my days.

I normalized them. That is what many of us do.

We normalize exhaustion. We normalize overwhelm. We normalize stress bragging. We normalize pushing through until our threshold for stress becomes our new baseline. Then one day, we realize that what we have been calling normal has been costing us more than we understood.

You do not have to be strong all the time to be worthy. You do not have to hold everything together to prove that you are capable. You are allowed to rest before your body forces you to.

You are allowed to take off the superwoman cape.

Because the same cape that convinces everyone you are okay can also hide the fact that you are falling apart.

So, before we go further, sit with your own experience. When was the last time you felt truly rested, not just physically, but mentally and emotionally? If you have found yourself tired in a way that rest does not fix, or disconnected in a way you cannot explain, what you are carrying may be more than ordinary stress. It may be burnout.

Burnout was not trying to destroy me.

It was trying to get my attention.

Chapter Summary

Burnout rarely announces itself. For me, it arrived quietly, disguised as ambition, discipline, and responsibility. It lived in a cluttered home I no longer had the energy to organize, in a body that stopped feeling rested no matter how much I slept, and in a professional life where I kept proving my relevance in a space I had already outgrown. I was still functioning. I was not well.

1. **Burnout is not a failure to cope.** It is a response to prolonged stress, and it often happens to people who handle pressure well, for far too long.
2. **Functioning is not the same as well-being.** You can meet every deadline, keep every commitment, and still be running on empty.
3. **Your environment often tells the truth first.** The clutter, the fog, the irritability, and the fatigue are not character flaws. They are information.
4. **Achievement can be driven by purpose or by pressure.** When our worth becomes chained to our output, ambition stops being a gift and starts becoming armor.
5. **Capacity is the real conversation.** We name what still has to get done. We rarely name how much room we have left to do it. Saying yes with no capacity is not commitment. It is depletion.
6. **Healing requires honest inventory.** Not only of our workload, but of our relationships. Some of what drains us never appears on a calendar.
7. **Awareness comes before strategy.** The question is not, *What is wrong with me?* The question is: *What have I been carrying simply because I am capable of carrying it?*

Hard Truth

> The loss of income did not create my burnout.
> It exposed what years of pushing through had allowed me to ignore.

CAPACITY CHECK

Write Your Own Unedited Version

Before you move into the next chapter, spend a few minutes with your own story. Not the version you would share in a meeting or post online. The honest one.

Chapter 2 will give you language for the quiet signs of burnout. These questions will help prepare you to recognize what may already be trying to get your attention.

Reflection Questions

1. What parts of my story did I recognize in this chapter, and what did it bring up for me?
2. What signs has my body been sending that I have minimized, ignored, or explained away?
3. What have I been calling ambition, discipline, or strength that may actually be survival?
4. When the pace of my life slows down, what thoughts, feelings, or truths become harder to avoid?
5. If I wrote the unedited version of the last two years of my life, what would I finally admit that I have not said out loud?

Chapter 2

Sis, You're Tired: The Quiet Signs You're Burning Out

"Burnout rarely announces itself with urgency.
It settles into your routine and becomes part of how you operate."
~ Dr. Tashina Reeder

Jada sat in her car a little longer than necessary, the engine off but her mind still running. Her laptop bag rested in the passenger seat, and her phone lit up continuously with notifications stacking faster than she could clear them. She had just finished a client call for one of her businesses, smiled on cue, and promised a "quick turnaround" she already knew was not going to be quick.

She opened her laptop and was instantly overwhelmed by the row of open tabs stretching across the top of the screen, each one a task still to be completed, each belonging to a different company she owned. She leaned her head back, closed her eyes, and whispered, "I'm tired." And still, she picked up her bag, went inside, and began to work some more.

Jada was a serial entrepreneur. On paper, that sounded impressive, and in some ways it was. She had built a consulting practice, a product line, and a small nonprofit she believed in deeply. What the title did not capture was that she was the entire team. She was the marketer, the bill collector, the customer service line, and the founder of all of it, wearing every hat for every business, all at once. She tried to focus on the one that brought in the most money, but the others still needed her, and there was only one of her.

Her water had gone warm an hour ago. She kept sipping it anyway, just to stay awake, just to keep going. Her shoulders ached. Her jaw was tight. She could not remember the last time she had taken a full, deep breath. Just as she exhaled, another message came through, marked urgent.

She had the capacity for the client call. She did not have the capacity for what came after it, and nobody had asked.

By 11:47 p.m., she was back on her laptop, keeping all of it running while her own rest stayed untouched in the background. The work came naturally to her. Boundaries did not. Her days blurred into deadlines, discovery calls, invoices, and revisions that were never as quick as they were described. She could not remember the last time she had taken a real vacation, because stepping away meant nothing got done and nothing came in. If she stopped, everything stopped. She invested in courses promising six-figure success yet struggled to secure a full night of sleep. From the outside, she appeared productive and successful. Internally, she was exhausted.

Somewhere in the middle of all of it, Jada also got quiet. Her group chat noticed before she did. She stopped responding to the daily memes. She let three separate invitations to brunch go unanswered, not because she did not want to see her friends, but because the thought of holding up her end of a conversation felt like one more task on a list that was already too long.

When she did show up, she found herself nodding along to conversations she was not fully following, laughing half a beat late, and hoping no one asked her a direct question. She told herself she was just tired. She did not yet have language for what was actually happening. Her brain was so overextended trying to keep everything else running that she did not have much left for connection.

If you are honest, you have probably had moments like the ones in Jada's story. Maybe not in your car, but in your office, your bathroom, or standing in your kitchen scrolling through your phone just to buy yourself a few seconds of quiet. You paused long enough to feel it, and then you kept going. Not because you felt better, but because you felt responsible.

Because there were still expectations to meet, roles to fulfill, and people depending on you. That is where burnout can begin. Not when everything falls apart, but when you learn how to keep going anyway, despite the stress, tension, and exhaustion.

In Chapter 1, I shared what burnout looked like for me. It began with patterns I had normalized, ways of pushing through, performing, and overriding what my body was trying to communicate. Looking back, the signs were there long before I had language for them. They showed up in my energy, my mood, and my ability to feel present. But because I was still functioning, I did not recognize them as warning signs. Jada's experience reflects that same pattern.

This is part of what makes burnout difficult to recognize. It rarely presents as an obvious disruption. More often, it develops gradually, working its way into your daily routines in ways that feel manageable at first. You may find yourself going through the motions, completing tasks without the same sense of connection you once had. Things that used to feel manageable may now feel heavier. Your patience may be shorter, your energy more inconsistent, and even rest may not leave you feeling restored.

Because you are still functioning, it becomes easy to dismiss what you are feeling. You tell yourself you are simply busy, that things will slow down eventually, or that you just need to get through this particular season. But for many women, that season does not pass. It stretches on and gradually becomes a way of life.

Over time, you may begin to notice subtle but significant changes. You are doing everything, yet enjoying very little. You are present in spaces, yet feel emotionally disconnected. You are productive, yet depleted. You are meeting expectations yet feel as though nothing you do is enough. You are there for everyone else, yet your own life feels chaotic.

This is the quiet nature of burnout. It does not always look like breaking down. Sometimes, it looks like holding everything together while quietly coming undone.

How Do You Know It's Burnout?

Before we go further, let's clarify what we mean by burnout. As shared in the introduction, the World Health Organization (WHO, 2019) identifies burnout as an occupational phenomenon resulting from chronic workplace stress that has not been successfully managed.

That is the clinical language. Within the broader lens of this book, here is the plain language: burnout is what happens when you have been giving more than you have been replenishing for so long that your mind, body, and emotions begin running on reserve.

It is not a personal failing, and it is not a lack of discipline. It can happen to capable people who keep going long after they need space to recover. Because so much of your life may be holding together, it is easy to overlook the signs or attribute them to temporary stress. But your body and mind are often communicating long before you are ready to listen.

Why These Signs Go Unnoticed

Burnout in high-achieving women is hard to see because the markers of success stay intact. The work still gets delivered. The people who depend on you are still taken care of. From the outside, nothing looks like it is falling apart, and that is exactly because you keep producing. What is being depleted does not show on the surface.

Capacity is invisible until it runs out.

Some of the behaviors that drain us are so ordinary, and so often praised, that we never think to question them. Read through the ones that follow and notice which feel familiar. Each one includes where it comes from and what it actually costs you.

1. **Perfectionism Masquerading as Excellence**

What it looks like: Hours spent refining minor details, rewriting the same email three times, delaying a project because it is not quite ready, and making sure every t is crossed and every i is dotted.

Where it comes from: Fear of failure, rejection, not being good enough, or being negatively perceived. People work hard to appear composed, capable, and in control because they fear what others might think if they are seen struggling, making a mistake, or falling short of the image they have worked so hard to maintain.

What it costs: The appearance of perfection has a price, and it is paid in capacity you never budgeted for. The work gets done either way. What changes is how much of you is left afterward.

2. **Over-Productivity as a Measure of Worth**

What it looks like: Feeling guilty for taking breaks, filling every gap in the calendar, and needing to feel busy in order to feel valuable or needed.

Where it comes from: Conditioning that ties your worth to productivity and praises constant doing over well-being.

What it costs: You begin measuring your value by how much you produce, pushing beyond your capacity and calling exhaustion discipline.

3. **Chronic Overcommitment**

What it looks like: Saying yes to every request, committee, favor, or extra project, even when you are already exhausted.

Where it comes from: It can be rooted in people-pleasing, the need for validation, or a learned fear that saying no will lead to judgment, rejection, or being seen as selfish, lazy, or ungrateful.

What it costs: Chronic overcommitment leaves you exhausted, resentful, and responsible for more than you have the capacity to carry. Saying yes without capacity is not commitment. It is depletion with a deadline attached.

4. **Emotional Eating and Overspending**

What it looks like: Reaching for food, opening the shopping app, or adding something else to the cart when the day has been long.

Where it comes from: A need for comfort, relief, or escape when you have no other place to put what you are feeling.

What it costs: Temporary relief can lead to weight changes, financial strain, and difficulty saving, while leaving the real need beneath the behavior unaddressed.

Taken individually, none of these choices look like a crisis: skipping lunch, sending one more email, saying yes to avoid the conversation that no would require, scrolling to numb something you have not named, or reaching for another cup of coffee instead of asking why you are so drained in the first place.

Each behavior may seem harmless on its own. But together, they can form an invisible pattern that slowly tightens around your time, your energy, and your sense of self. None of them looks like a crisis, yet each one quietly drains capacity you may not realize you are spending.

I once worked with a woman who was the person everyone called. She organized everything, remembered what others forgot, and always showed up when someone needed her. But at night, when no one was asking anything more of her, she would binge-watch television until two in the morning, eat whatever was quickest, and fill an online shopping cart she rarely checked out. She called those nights her bad habits.

They were not bad habits. They were coping tools. They were doing what she needed them to do in that moment: helping her escape, numb out, and find a little relief after spending the entire day being everything for everyone else. By the time she reached for them, her capacity was already depleted, but the demands had never stopped.

These are the ordinary behaviors. Underneath them, burnout is speaking in ways that are easier to feel than to name.

How Burnout Speaks

Emotional Signs

One of the most common signs of burnout is emotional exhaustion. This is not simply feeling tired after a long day. It is a deeper depletion, where even small tasks begin to feel overwhelming. You may notice that your patience is shorter, your tolerance is lower, and your ability to engage emotionally feels limited. Conversations may feel draining rather than connecting. Situations that once felt manageable may now feel like too much.

Another quiet sign is a sense of detachment or disconnection. You may find yourself going through the motions without feeling fully present. This can show up at work, in your relationships, or even in moments that are supposed to bring joy. You are there, but something feels distant. This experience is often described in research as depersonalization, in which individuals create emotional distance as a way to cope with ongoing stress (Maslach & Leiter, 2016). In plain terms, this means you can be sitting right in the middle of your own life, present in the room, technically available, while some part of you has already checked out. It is not that you stopped caring. It is that caring, right now, costs more than you have to spend.

Burnout can also impact your sense of effectiveness. You may begin to question whether what you are doing is enough, even when you are accomplishing a great deal. Tasks may take longer to complete, not because you are incapable, but because your mental and emotional capacity is stretched. Over time, this can lead to procrastination and a reduced sense of accomplishment, where nothing feels satisfying no matter how much you get done.

Emotionally, you may also notice increased irritability, frustration, or even numbness. There may be moments where you feel overwhelmed, pressured to perform or know all the answers, followed by moments where you feel disconnected from everything. This fluctuation can be confusing, especially when you are used to being consistent and in control.

Physical Signs

Physical signs can also be easy to overlook. Chronic fatigue, headaches, muscle tension (you know, the kind of tension that somehow has your shoulder muscles touching the bottom of your earlobes from carrying so much stress), disrupted sleep, and weight gain or loss may all be connected to prolonged stress. For some people, chronic stress can also show up as hair loss, restlessness, or feeling more anxious or on edge.

It helps to be clear about the direction here. Burnout does not cause these things. Chronic stress does, and burnout is what develops when that stress goes unmanaged for too long. These signs are not proof that you are burned out either, and they can have many other causes, so they are worth bringing to your doctor.

Researchers describe the accumulated wear and tear of ongoing stress as allostatic load, the toll it takes on the body over time (McEwen, 2007). Over the long term, that toll has been linked to more serious health risks, including cardiovascular disease. We will look more closely at what chronic stress does to the body, and why it lands harder on some of us than others, in the next chapter.

The body responds to ongoing pressure by remaining in a heightened state of alert, which can make it harder to fully recover over time. When rest no longer feels restorative, or you wake up still feeling exhausted, it may be a sign that your body has not fully come out of that stress response. Over time, you can begin functioning on autopilot, continuing to move through your responsibilities even while your body is signaling that it needs something different.

Cognitive Signs

Cognitively, burnout can show up as difficulty concentrating, forgetfulness, or what many describe as "brain fog." You may find it harder to focus, retain information, make decisions, or organize your thoughts in the way you normally would.

Things that once felt simple can begin to require more mental effort. You may read the same paragraph several times and still not remember what you just read. You may walk into a room and forget why you went there, lose your train of thought in the middle of a sentence, or struggle to find a word that you know you know. Even making small decisions can begin to feel overwhelming when your mind is already carrying too much.

Sometimes it can feel as though your brain is moving more slowly than the rest of your life. You are still showing up, still working, still responding to people, but mentally, you may feel a step behind. That can be frustrating, especially when you are accustomed to being sharp, organized, and able to think quickly.

These changes do not necessarily mean that you have suddenly become less capable. They may be signs that your mind has been operating under prolonged stress without enough opportunity to recover. When your mental capacity is stretched for too long, even ordinary thinking can begin to feel like work.

Cognitive Signs of Burnout

1. Difficulty concentrating
2. Forgetfulness
3. Brain fog
4. Trouble making decisions
5. Slower thinking
6. Losing your train of thought
7. Difficulty finding the right words
8. Feeling mentally "offline"

9. Struggling to follow conversations

A systematic review and meta-analysis of clinical burnout found measurable impairments across several of these domains, including attention, processing speed, working memory, and executive function (Gavelin et al., 2022). This is not a character flaw, and it is not a sign that you are somehow less capable than you used to be. It is what happens when your brain has been running in a heightened state for too long without enough recovery in between.

Social Signs

This brings me to another sign that often gets misread, and I want to name it clearly because I think a lot of us have judged ourselves for it. Burnout does not necessarily make you socially awkward. It can make you socially depleted. Those are not the same thing, and the difference matters.

Social awkwardness can feel like something is wrong with who you are or how you interact with others. Social depletion is different. It is not about who you are. It is about how much capacity you have left to show up the way you normally would.

Think of your brain like a phone sitting at two percent battery. Someone running on that little charge is spending nearly everything they have just to get through the day, the meetings, the deadlines, and the version of themselves everyone else is depending on. That does not leave much left over for following a conversation, finding the right word, catching a joke, remembering what someone just said, or making small talk at the mailbox.

So, you may come across as quiet, distant, a little "off," maybe even uninterested. But what is happening on the inside is closer to: *I cannot keep up with this conversation,* or *I know what I want to say, and I cannot get my brain to cooperate long enough to say it.*

There was a time when I began to think I was becoming socially awkward because I did not have the mental capacity for conversations that required deeper thought. I would listen, observe, and then suddenly lose track of what was being said. Sometimes my mind would simply freeze, leaving me unable to find the words or follow the conversation.

It felt so unlike me that I actually called two of my friends and asked them if they experienced me as socially awkward. I needed to know if they were noticing something I was noticing in myself. I had never known myself to be socially awkward, so feeling this different and this socially disconnected was strange to me. I knew I was capable of engaging, but in those moments, I simply did not have enough mental capacity left to do it the way I normally would.

That experience was unsettling, but it was not a reflection of my intelligence or ability. It was a sign of how much mental strain I had been carrying for far too long. What I had interpreted as becoming socially awkward was, in many ways, social depletion. I was not losing who I was. I was running out of the capacity I needed to fully show up as myself.

Social Signs of Burnout

1. Withdrawing from people
2. Avoiding phone calls and texts
3. Declining invitations
4. Feeling emotionally unavailable
5. Becoming quieter than usual
6. Feeling disconnected during conversations
7. Feeling like socializing requires too much effort

Research backs this up. One study that re-examined the core symptoms of burnout found that social withdrawal showed up as one of its defining features, right alongside exhaustion and cognitive impairment. People experiencing burnout tended to become more insular, pulling back from social interaction even when they were not consciously choosing to (Tavella et al., 2021).

This is exactly what was happening with Jada in that group chat. She had not changed as a person. Her capacity had changed for a season.

I think that distinction matters, because so many of us have told ourselves the same story: that we have somehow become harder to be around, less fun, less present, less ourselves. That is rarely what is happening. What is usually closer to the truth is this: your mind no longer has the capacity to engage the way it once did, not because you stopped caring about people, but because caring takes energy you have not had in a while.

Environmental Signs

There is another category of burnout that often gets overlooked because it does not happen inside your body first. It happens around you. Sometimes burnout leaves clues in your environment long before you are willing to admit something is wrong.

You may notice dishes sitting in the sink longer than usual, laundry piling up, unopened mail collecting on the counter, or paperwork slowly taking over your desk. Your car may become more cluttered. The room you keep saying you will organize "this weekend" somehow never gets done. You tell yourself you just need to catch up, but catching up never quite happens.

This is not necessarily laziness or poor housekeeping. It is often a reflection of diminished mental and emotional capacity.

Psychologists have long understood that our environments and our emotional well-being influence one another. When the brain is overwhelmed by chronic stress, it naturally begins conserving energy for what feels most essential. Tasks that require planning, organization, and sustained attention, such as cleaning, sorting, or putting things away, often become more difficult because those same executive functioning skills are already depleted by burnout (McEwen, 2007; Gavelin et al., 2022). Research on home environments has found a similar pattern, linking the state of a person's living space to daily shifts in mood and stress hormones (Saxbe & Repetti, 2010).

Sometimes the clutter is not the problem. It is a signal that something else may be going on underneath.

Your environment may begin reflecting what your nervous system has been carrying for months.

Environmental Signs of Burnout

1. Clutter accumulating in your home
2. Laundry or dishes piling up
3. Paperwork, unopened mail, or unfinished projects stacking up
4. A workspace that becomes increasingly disorganized
5. A cluttered vehicle
6. Frequently moving clutter from one place to another without actually organizing it
7. Difficulty starting or finishing household tasks
8. Feeling overwhelmed by the thought of cleaning or organizing
9. Losing motivation to maintain spaces that once brought you peace
10. Feeling embarrassed for people to see your home

One of the more subtle signs of burnout is that your environment begins to tell the story your body has been trying to tell you all along. Many people describe feeling ashamed of the clutter without realizing that the clutter itself may be communicating something important. Instead of asking, "Why can't I keep up?" a more compassionate question might be, "What has been taking so much of my energy that there hasn't been enough left for this?"

Pause here for a second. Inhale and exhale.

If you have read this far and found yourself nodding, that is not a coincidence. That is recognition. You do not need to check every box on every list to know something is off. Even one is enough to pay attention to.

But meeting expectations is not the same as thriving. And there is a version of your life where you get to do both.

Research supports this experience. Burnout is characterized by three primary dimensions: emotional exhaustion, depersonalization, and a reduced sense of personal accomplishment (Maslach & Leiter, 2016). You have just read what each of those looks like from the inside. This is why awareness matters, because the quiet signs are often the first indicators that something needs to shift.

You do not have to wait until you are overwhelmed to acknowledge that something is off.

The driving force matters as much as the load. What exhausts you is not only what you carry, but how long you have been carrying it without the support, space, or recovery you need.

And if you are honest, you have likely noticed at least one of these signs. Maybe more.

Chapter Summary

Burnout rarely announces itself. It settles into the routine and becomes part of how you operate. Jada was still delivering, still showing up, still doing the work well. What had changed was not her ability. It was how much room she had left.

1. **The quiet signs are the early signs.** Burnout does not always interrupt your life. More often it shifts how you think, how you feel, and how you move through your day, while everything on paper still looks fine.
2. **Burnout speaks in more than one language.** It shows up emotionally, physically, cognitively, socially, and in your environment. You do not have to recognize yourself in every category for it to be real.
3. **Social depletion is not social awkwardness.** Pulling back from people is rarely about who you have become. It is about how much you have left to give a conversation.
4. **Your environment tells the truth early.** The clutter, the piles, the room you keep meaning to get to are often the first place diminished capacity becomes visible.
5. **Every quiet sign is a capacity signal.** The behaviors are not the problem. They are the receipt. Each one is telling you what you have already spent.
6. **Noticing is not the same as diagnosing.** You do not need every box checked to take this seriously. One is enough to pay attention to.
7. **Meeting expectations is not the same as thriving.** You can do everything right and still be running on reserve. There is a version of your life where you get to do both.

The signs were never the problem. They were the invitation.

Hard Truth

> Burnout is not the problem. It is the warning sign.
> Are you paying attention?

CAPACITY CHECK

Notice What Resonated

Take a moment to sit with what you have just read.

Burnout often hides in routines and patterns that have become familiar. This chapter is an invitation to notice what may have been normalized in your own life.

Consider the moments when something felt off, but you continued anyway. The times you dismissed your exhaustion, minimized your stress, or told yourself to push through. Awareness begins when you allow yourself to acknowledge those experiences without judgment.

Ask yourself: What have I been calling normal?

Questions

1. Where did I see myself in this chapter?
2. What signs of burnout have I been overlooking or minimizing?
3. What have I been treating as normal that is quietly draining me?
4. When was the last time I felt mentally and emotionally restored?
5. What is one pattern I can now recognize more clearly?

PHASE II:

THE SOUL SHIFT

Understanding What's Beneath the Burnout

"Do the best you can until you know better.
Then when you know better, do better."

~ Dr. Maya Angelou

Chapter 3

Why We Push Past Our Limits

The Patterns, Pressure, and the Achievement Trap

"Govern your life by priorities, not your pressures."
~ Dr. Myles Munroe

"I'll rest when things slow down." Danielle said it without thinking, scrolling through emails with one hand while reheating her coffee for the third time. The day had barely started, and she was already behind on tasks she never had time to catch up on in the first place.

By 7:45 a.m., she had answered three work emails from bed, packed two lunches, found her son's missing shin guard, and mentally rearranged her Thursday to make room for a client call before her actual job even started. Danielle works a full nine-to-five, the kind with a badge, a boss, and a calendar full of other people's priorities. But by six o'clock, she becomes someone else entirely: the owner of a small business she built from nothing, squeezed into early mornings, lunch breaks, and the hour after everyone else falls asleep.

She is the marketer, the bookkeeper, the customer service line, and the one who packages every order herself because she cannot yet afford to pay someone else to. She is also a wife and a mother of two, the one who remembers the pediatrician's number by heart and keeps the family calendar in her head, because writing it all down would mean admitting how much of it there actually is. Her husband asks what is for dinner. Her son asks where his cleats are. Her business asks for content she has not had the bandwidth to create in eleven days. And somewhere in the middle of all of it is Danielle, who has not asked herself a single question about what she needs since sometime around March.

Meetings stack on meetings. Messages are marked urgent. People need something, everyone needs something, and Danielle says yes to nearly all of it, because saying no has never felt like an option available to her. She paused briefly at her desk, just long enough to notice the tightness in her chest, the way it climbed up into her throat and sat there. She pressed a hand flat against her sternum, breathed, and kept going. "I'll rest later." Later, however, had been coming for years.

Earlier that morning she had read the same message four times before answering it, softening a line, then softening it again, making sure it did not sound short. It took eleven minutes she did not have, for a reply nobody would remember by lunch.

By the time her paid workday began, Danielle had already spent an hour of capacity she would never get back. Nobody counted that hour. Including her.

Many high-achieving women repeat this same internal script, promising rest as if it waits somewhere in the future, at a finish line that never quite arrives.

Let's be honest. You have said the same thing. You have treated rest like a reward instead of a requirement, something to be earned rather than something you inherently need. Not because something is wrong with you, but because you were never taught how to rest.

The tendency to push beyond personal limits is often framed as ambition or discipline. In reality, it more accurately reflects a conditioned behavioral and psychological response. Many women have been socialized to keep going regardless of internal signals, praised for perseverance, rewarded for overperformance, and affirmed for being dependable. Over time, this reinforcement makes slowing down feel unfamiliar, uncomfortable, and, in some cases, unsafe.

This chapter is not here to judge how you got here. It is here to help you understand why. And understanding is where everything begins to shift.

The Psychology of Pushing Through

The Achievement Spectrum: High Achiever vs. Overachiever

Not all achievement is created equal. From the outside, high achievers and overachievers can look exactly the same. Both are productive, driven, and capable. Both meet expectations and often exceed them. Both are praised, promoted, and relied upon. But the difference is not in what they do. The difference is in why they do it.

A Closer Look at the Difference

Everything that separates them is underneath. Hold this comparison in mind as you read the rest of this section, because the pages that follow are an unpacking of it.

Traits	The High Achiever (Internally Driven)	The Overachiever (Externally Driven)
What Drives Her	Purpose, growth, curiosity	Validation, fear of inadequacy and judgement.
How She Works	Works hard, then recovers.	Works hard, then works harder.
Relationship With Rest	Rest is part of the plan.	Rest must be earned, and rarely is.
After Reaching a Goal	Pauses, celebrates, absorbs it.	Moves immediately to the next thing.
Identity and Self-Worth	Relatively stable, separate from output.	Tied to achievement, rises and falls with it.

Relationship to Capacity	Works within it, treats limits as information.	Overrides it, treats limits as failure.
Risk of Burnout	Lower when boundaries hold	High, from chronic overextension

A high achiever is driven by purpose and internal motivation. Her work is connected to her values and a genuine sense of direction. Rest, while not always prioritized, is still accessible. She can step away without feeling like her identity is at risk.

An overachiever is driven by pressure, fear, and internalized expectation. Achievement becomes a way to secure worth, avoid failure, or maintain control, so there is no real finish line. The moment one goal is met, anxiety pushes her toward the next, and rest feels not neutral but undeserved, even unsafe.

Let me give you two women so you can see yourself in this more clearly.

The purpose-driven achiever launches her business because she genuinely believes in the work and feels called to serve in that way. When challenges arise, she reassesses, adjusts, and keeps going with resilience. She celebrates milestones. She delegates when needed. She rests because she understands that sustainability is part of the strategy. When she is not working, she can be present with the people she loves without her mind racing through her task list.

The fear-driven achiever launches that same business, but the engine underneath is different. She is working to prove something, to herself, to people who doubted her, to the version of her younger self who felt overlooked or not enough. Every achievement temporarily quiets the fear, but it never eliminates it. So she keeps going, harder and faster, because stopping feels like losing. She does not know how to celebrate because she is already onto the next thing. She does not delegate because asking for help feels scary. She cannot control the narrative once it leaves her hands, so it feels safer to just do it herself,

because somewhere underneath, she believes that if she doesn't do it, it won't get done, or won't get done correctly.

She does not rest because rest means she might have to sit with the voice that says she is still not doing enough. Both women are working. Both women are achieving. But only one of them is actually living.

Research on motivation offers important clinical context here. Self-determination theory differentiates between intrinsic motivation, driven by internal values and genuine interest, and controlled motivation, driven by external pressure, fear, or the need for approval (Ryan & Deci, 2017). High achievers tend to operate from intrinsic motivation. Overachievers often operate from controlled motivation, even when the external rewards appear identical. This distinction matters because it determines how burnout develops. When you are driven by purpose, you can endure difficulty without losing yourself. When you are driven by fear, even success becomes exhausting.

Research on perfectionism deepens this understanding. Maladaptive perfectionism, closely associated with overachievement, has been consistently linked to higher levels of anxiety (Smith et al., 2018), and the broader perfectionism literature connects it to depression and burnout as well. This form of striving is not about excellence. It is about avoiding the perceived failure or inadequacy that lives just one misstep away.

It is also important to understand that these are not rigid categories. You can be both. Many women move between high achievement and overachievement depending on the season, the relationship, or the circumstance. You may feel aligned and grounded in one area of your life while feeling pressured and overextended in another. The same person can operate from purpose in one season and from survival in another. That does not make you inconsistent. It makes you human.

The goal is not to eliminate ambition. The goal is to become aware of what is driving it. Because when your achievement is rooted in fear, it will always cost you more than it gives you. And when it is rooted in alignment, it becomes something you can actually sustain.

The Wound Beneath the Drive

If the last section held up a mirror, this one is going to ask you to look a little deeper. Because understanding the difference between high achievement and overachievement is one thing. Understanding why so many women find themselves living in that second category is another conversation entirely. In many cases, overachievement is not simply ambition. It is a trauma response.

Trauma: the emotional, psychological, or physical impact of an experience that overwhelms a person's ability to cope. Trauma is not defined only by what happened, but by how the experience affected the mind, body, and nervous system. What feels traumatic for one person may not feel traumatic for another because each person's experiences and resources are different (Substance Abuse and Mental Health Services Administration, 2014).

A trauma response: the body's automatic reaction to a real or perceived threat. It is an unconscious survival response designed to protect you from danger, even when the original threat has passed. These responses can include fighting, fleeing, freezing, or people-pleasing (fawning), and often occur before you have time to think logically (van der Kolk, 2014).

Research in trauma psychology suggests that when individuals grow up in environments where love, approval, or safety feel conditional, they may develop performance-based identities, using achievement as a way to secure worth (LePera, 2021). When parental or caregiver affection depends on a child's achievement, it cultivates a looming fear of failure and deeply ingrained perfectionism (Assor & Tal, 2012). You learn early on that you are loved for what you produce, not simply for who you are.

In this context, success does not just feel good. Success becomes a strategy for survival.

That means somewhere in your story, you learned that being productive, capable, reliable, and impressive was not just a good quality to have. It was a way to stay safe. It was a way to belong. It was a way to earn the love, the approval, or the stability you needed and were not sure you could access any other way. You performed your way into safety. And it worked.

The problem is that survival strategies do not come with an expiration date. Nobody tells your nervous system when the original threat is gone. So you keep achieving, keep producing, keep performing, long after the environment that required it has changed.

What once protected you may now be exhausting you. Because surviving is not the same as living.

Let's talk about what this actually looks like.

Fear of failure shows up as the woman who cannot submit work until it is perfect, who rewrites the same email five times, who lies awake running through scenarios of what could go wrong. The fear is not really about the work. It is about what failure means about her. Fear of rejection looks like the woman who says yes before anyone has to ask twice, who is available even when she is depleted, who softens every boundary before she even sets it because she cannot risk someone being disappointed in her.

Fear of being overlooked looks like the woman who volunteers for every committee, takes on every project, says yes to every invitation, not because she wants all of it, but because she is terrified that if she becomes invisible, she becomes dispensable.

Fear of not being enough looks like the woman who compares herself constantly, who downplays her accomplishments, who cannot receive a compliment without immediately redirecting it, who quietly believes that everything she has built is a few missteps away from being exposed as a mistake.

These are not personality flaws. They are the emotional residue of experiences that taught you worth must be earned, rest must be deserved, and performance is protection.

Physiologically, these patterns are reinforced through chronic stress exposure. Research on the body's cumulative stress load demonstrates that repeated activation of the stress response system recalibrates the body to function in a constant state of alertness (McEwen, 2007). Over time, high activity feels normal, while stillness feels unfamiliar or even unsafe. Your nervous system has adapted to the pace of performing. Slowing down does not feel like relief. It feels like a threat.

Emotional suppression compounds this effect. When feelings are consistently minimized or avoided, they do not disappear. They are carried within the body. Research shows that emotional suppression is associated with increased physiological stress responses and prolonged nervous system activation (Gross & Levenson, 1997). In other words, what you do not process, your body holds.

Taken together, these factors create a powerful and deeply personal pattern. And before we go any further, I want to name something clearly: these patterns are not random. They make sense. You did what you had to do to survive. But what helped you survive may not be what helps you live.

Where Over-Functioning Gets Learned

Over-functioning does not come from nowhere. It gets learned, usually early, and usually in response to something real.

Some of us learned it as the daughter who figured out that excelling was how to get noticed in a house where attention was scarce. She became accomplished because accomplishment worked, and she is still reaching for it now, still waiting to feel seen.

Some of us learned it as the first in the family to make it. She carries expectations that were never spoken out loud but were always understood, and she is praised for her drive by people who cannot see what it costs her to maintain it.

You may recognize one of these. You may recognize both, or neither, and something else entirely instead. The specifics matter less than the pattern underneath them, which is this: each of these women learned what she was supposed to carry long before anyone asked what she had the capacity to carry. Most of us were never asked at all. And after a while, we stopped asking ourselves. There is one more thing those learned patterns leave behind. A voice.

The Voice That Keeps Score

Most of us have a running commentary we rarely question.

I should be further along by now.

If I slow down, I will fall behind.

Do not ask for help. People will disappoint me and are unreliable.

If I don't do it, it won't get done correctly.

This voice is often shaped by authority figures, cultural narratives, and institutional norms that equate worth with constant productivity. You met mine in Chapter 1, in a professor's office, telling me I was not graduate school material. I carried that voice for years and mistook it for my own.

Notice what is missing from every one of those sentences. Not one of them asks what you have left. The inner critic only ever measures output.

The Cost of the Performance

There is a particular kind of exhaustion that comes from continually presenting a curated version of yourself to meet external expectations, often at the expense of your authenticity. It is not the work that wears you down. It is the maintenance of the image the work requires.

Performance fatigue is what happens when you spend capacity on an image you then have to keep maintaining. It is the one expense nobody budgets for, because it does not look like work. It looks like being fine.

Two Patterns That Keep the Cycle Running

Two more patterns belong here, not because they are symptoms, but because they are causes. They keep everything else in place.

1. **Hyper-Independence.** Refusing help. Saying I have got it before anyone finishes offering. Struggling to delegate even when you are underwater. It is usually rooted in having been let down, or in learning early that needing someone was not safe. Doing it all yourself does not increase your capacity. It only hides how far past it you already are.

2. **Lack of Self-Compassion.** Speaking to yourself in a tone you would never use with someone you love. Self-judgment is not free. It runs constantly in the background, and it draws from the same reserve everything else does.

Everything so far has been about patterns you can see in your day. Now we go underneath them, to what your body is doing while you run them.

When Stress Becomes a Trigger: Trauma Responses and the Burnout Cycle

Not all stress is created equal. For many high-achieving women, what looks like a response to a deadline or a difficult conversation is actually something deeper: a trauma response. As discussed earlier, when the nervous system learns that performance creates safety, it often responds to present-day stress as though old threats still exist.

Research in trauma psychology identifies this as a conditioned stress response, a pattern in which current stressors activate historical wounds, producing a reaction disproportionate to the present moment (van der Kolk, 2014). The overfunctioning, the inability to rest, the compulsive need to stay productive even when exhausted: these are not character flaws. They are the body remembering what it learned to feel safe.

We often talk about fight, flight, and freeze as trauma responses. But for many high-achieving women, survival takes a fourth form that rarely gets named. Coined by therapist Pete Walker, the fawn response is a trauma-driven pattern of people-pleasing and appeasement, activated when fighting, fleeing, or freezing do not feel safe or available (Walker, 2013). Overachievement and overfunctioning often function as fight or fawn responses. You fight off the threat of failure by working harder. You fawn by making sure everyone else is taken care of, perfectly, reliably, without complaint, so you will not be rejected, criticized, or let go. Both look like dedication from the outside. Both are survival responses on the inside.

The trigger is rarely dramatic. Something activates your internal alarm: a deadline, a tone of voice, a memory the body recognizes before the mind does, and your body responds first. Which of these four you reach for is not a choice you make. It is a pattern that was set long ago.

RESPONSE	WHAT IT DOES	WHAT IT LOOKS LIKE	THE BELIEF UNDERNEATH
FIGHT *Push Harder*	Mobilize to overpower the threat	Works longer and harder. Overdelivers to prove her worth. Cannot delegate. Pushes through exhaustion.	*I have to do this, or everything falls apart.*
FLIGHT *Escape And Avoid*	Mobilize to outrun the threat.	Avoids difficult tasks. Stays constantly busy. Jumps between projects. Struggles to be still.	*If I keep moving, I do not have to feel it.*
FREEZE *Shut Down*	Immobilize when escape is not possible.	Cannot start tasks. Feels numb or detached. Appears calm but is stuck. Dissociates under pressure.	*I know what I need to do. I just cannot move.*
FAWN *Please And Appease*	Merge with others to stay safe.	Says yes when she means no. Overachieves for approval. Puts everyone else first. Loses touch with her own needs.	*If I keep everyone happy, I will be safe.*

None of this is a matter of willpower. When burnout feels relentless, it is often because the nervous system is still responding to a threat that technically ended but was never fully resolved in the body.

This is also why burnout, for many women, does not feel like simple exhaustion. It feels like urgency. Like something will fall apart if you stop.

That feeling is not coming from your calendar. It is coming from your history.

Recognizing this is not meant to send you into an excavation of every difficult thing you have experienced. It is meant to give you permission to be curious rather than critical when your responses feel bigger than the moment seems to warrant. Your reactions make sense. They were learned. And what was learned can, over time, be unlearned, or at minimum, interrupted.

A Note for Black Women

This book is for all women, every woman who is tired, carrying too much, or quietly unraveling behind her accomplishments. Within that truth, however, there is something important to acknowledge. Black women often carry an additional layer of stress that accelerates burnout. We are among the most educated demographics in this country, and we continue to show up as entrepreneurs, leaders, caregivers, community pillars, and culture builders. We exist in spaces that require excellence, resilience, and adaptability, often all at the same time, and still, we are expected to keep going.

Too often, we run on fumes while performing a version of strength we do not always feel. We have learned how to show up even when we are not okay, how to continue producing even when we are exhausted, and how to carry what was never meant to be carried alone. I know this truth personally as a Black, educated, high-achieving woman of mature age who has lived through the weight of these expectations. This is not an abstract concept. It is lived, embodied, and deeply understood.

Researchers have described this pattern as the Strong Black Woman trope, also called the Superwoman trope, a cultural expectation that Black women remain resilient, self-sacrificing, emotionally contained, and capable regardless of the circumstances they face (Woods-Giscombé, 2010). While these qualities have often been necessary for survival, they can also make it profoundly difficult to acknowledge pain, ask for support, or prioritize rest. In one study, nearly 80% of the Black women surveyed identified with this cultural trope, which is linked to emotional suppression and heightened risk for depression (Abrams et al., 2019).

What is praised as strength can sometimes become a barrier to healing. This does not mean strength is the problem. The problem arises when strength becomes the only acceptable option. When vulnerability feels unsafe, asking for help feels burdensome, and rest feels undeserved, the very qualities that once supported survival can quietly contribute to burnout.

In the aftermath of the 2024 presidential election, a movement emerged among Black women that came to be known as the 92 Percent movement, named for the roughly 92% of Black women voters who, according to exit polls, had cast their ballots for the same candidate after organizing and showing up with everything they had. What is worth sitting with here, in a chapter about why we push past our limits, is what that movement actually was underneath the headlines.

It was not a withdrawal. It was a refusal, collectively and publicly, to keep pouring from an empty vessel in a culture that has expected Black women to pour indefinitely, regardless of the cost (Chisolm, 2024). Choosing rest, out loud and without apology, was the exact opposite of everything this chapter has described: the overfunctioning, the earned rest, the belief that stopping means everything falls apart.

What struck many observers, and what felt deeply resonant to women far beyond the Black community, was the permission embedded in that moment. Watching Black women choose themselves, unapologetically and out loud, gave other women quiet language for something they had been feeling but had not yet said. If they could sit down after carrying all of that, maybe I am also allowed to rest. The 92 Percent movement was not just a cultural moment. It was a mirror. And what it reflected was a truth that this entire book is built on: rest is not weakness. Rest is wisdom. And sometimes, the most radical thing a woman can do is simply stop, and let that be enough. Or, in the words of the Black culture: rest is tea.

You will not find pathology or blame here. You will find compassion, acknowledgment, and space to exhale. Because you deserve spaces where you do not have to be strong all the time. For many Black women, this is not where the story begins. It is where it continues. The pressure to be strong, to endure, and to achieve despite barriers is not only individually learned. It is culturally and historically reinforced.

Patterns of resilience, overfunctioning, and emotional suppression are often passed down, not simply through instruction, but through lived example and modeled survival. This is what intergenerational transmission looks like in real time. You are not only carrying your own expectations. You are carrying what was never safe for the women before you to put down.

That same truth about rest and permission surfaced again when former First Lady Michelle Obama openly explained why she had chosen not to attend a high-profile public event that tradition and expectation had long required of women in her position. Speaking on her podcast IMO in April 2025, Obama described the internal struggle of choosing herself over what was perceived as right. Her guest, actress Taraji P. Henson, named something many women will feel immediately: that when a woman does not make choices for herself, she becomes a shock absorber for everyone around her, and that carrying that role for everyone else is exhausting and unhealthy (Obama & Robinson, 2025).

What made that conversation particularly striking was not just the decision itself. It was the public response to it. People could not accept that a woman, even one of the most accomplished and visible women in the world, was simply choosing her own well-being. Obama noted that her absence generated so much speculation that people assumed her marriage was falling apart, because a grown woman making a set of decisions for herself did not fit the story people expected.

That reaction tells us everything. It tells us how deeply the expectation of women's constant availability is embedded in our culture, and how countercultural it still feels when a woman simply says: not this time. I am choosing me.

It is important to name that this makes sense. The version of you that learned how to perform, produce, and persevere was adaptive, resourceful, and effective. She is not the problem. However, adaptation is not the same as sustainability. The strategies that once protected you may not be the ones that sustain you long-term. That version of you deserves gratitude, not shame. She got you here.

And if you sit with that truth long enough, it can bring up something deeper than understanding. It can bring up grief. Grief for how long you have been carrying what was never meant to be carried alone. Grief for the times you had to be strong when you needed support. Grief for the version of you who learned to earn love, safety, and belonging through performance instead of simply being.

This is also where the shift begins. You are no longer in the same place you were when you first learned those patterns. You have awareness now, and awareness creates choice. You now have the opportunity to decide whether you will continue living from survival or begin living from alignment. You get to choose whether your worth remains tied to what you do or becomes grounded in who you are. You get to choose whether rest is something you must earn or something you allow yourself to receive.

What protected you then is not what will sustain you now.

Your healing is not about becoming someone new. It is about releasing what you no longer have to carry so that you can finally live as yourself.

Hard Truth

The drive that is burning you out once kept you safe. That is why willpower alone has never been enough to stop it.

Chapter Summary

Danielle had not failed at managing her time. She was running a pattern she learned long before she had a say in it, and that pattern had a name she had never been given: she was living past her capacity and calling it responsibility.

1. **Ambition is not the problem**. What drives it is. The high achiever and the overachiever are almost impossible to tell apart from the outside. The difference is whether the engine underneath is purpose or fear.
2. **Overachievement is often a survival strategy.** When love, approval, or safety felt conditional, performance became the way to secure them. It worked once, which is exactly why it is so hard to put down.
3. **Survival strategies have no expiration date.** Nobody tells your nervous system the original threat has passed, so you keep performing long after the danger is gone.
4. **The inner critic only measures output.** It will tell you to move faster, do more, and ask for less. It will never once ask what you have left.
5. **The drive is not your enemy, and it is not who you are.** It is something you learned, which means it is something you can begin to hold differently.

The strategy that kept you safe is not the one that will carry you forward.

CAPACITY CHECK

Look Underneath

Take a moment to sit with what came up for you in this chapter. Not to fix it. Not to overanalyze it. Just to notice it.

On the Psychology of Pushing Through

1. When I think about my achievements, what is typically driving me: purpose or pressure?
2. When did I first learn that I had to keep going, no matter what?
3. What am I afraid would happen if I slowed down?

Chapter 4

The Systems That Keep Us Stuck

Roles, Labor, and Hustle Culture

"Caring for myself is not self-indulgence; it is self-preservation, and that is an act of political warfare."
~ Audre Lorde

Renata kept a running list in her head that never actually ended. Not on paper, because paper would have meant she could put it down. It lived behind everything else she did: the permission slip due Friday, her mother's refill that needed calling in, the coworker out on leave, and the report that would land on her because she was the one who always caught it. She was good at holding it. That was the problem. She had become so good at holding it that no one, including her, could see how much she was carrying.

Nobody had assigned her the list. It had accumulated the way these things do, one reasonable request at a time, each one small enough to say yes to, until the sum of them was a second full-time job that existed nowhere except inside her. At work she was the dependable one. At home she was the one who remembered. In her family she was the one who managed. None of it had a title. None of it showed up on a review or a paycheck. And all of it was hers.

This is the part of burnout that the last chapter could not fully explain. Danielle's exhaustion came from the engine inside her, the drive, the wound, the voice that kept score. But not all of it starts on the inside. Some of it is built into the rooms you walk into, the roles you are handed, and a culture that calls your depletion ambition and then hands you more.

The Systems That Sustain the Cycle

This pattern does not exist in isolation. It is shaped by the systems in which individuals operate. The traditional work structure prioritizes productivity, efficiency, and output, often at the expense of emotional and physical well-being. While benefits such as paid time off may exist, they are frequently tied to approval processes and organizational demands that do not align with personal capacity. Asking for permission to rest is rarely restorative.

Research indicates that high job demands, low autonomy, and limited psychological safety significantly increase burnout and emotional exhaustion (Maslach & Leiter, 2016). When individuals do not feel safe acknowledging overwhelm, they are more likely to remain in a prolonged state of stress activation. That stress does not remain confined to the workplace. It follows you home, into your conversations, your relationships, and the moments that are supposed to be quiet.

After a full day of performing, producing, and managing expectations, many women transition into another set of responsibilities. Caregiving, partnership, and household demands extend the same internal dialogue: we will handle it, we will push through, we will rest later. Over time, delayed rest becomes depletion.

Chronic stress exposure has been consistently linked to increased risk of physical illness, anxiety, and depression when recovery is postponed (McEwen, 2007). When you feel emotionally drained, physically exhausted, or mentally overwhelmed, it is not random. It is cumulative. It is the cost of repeatedly overriding your need for rest.

The Beliefs That Keep You Moving

One of the beliefs that keeps you overextending is the belief that something has to be done before you are allowed to pause, that you have to produce your way into a break. Many individuals were raised in environments where productivity was praised, and stillness was questioned. Cultural messages such as "finish your work first, and then…", "You are bored, you must need something to do." or "do not be lazy" contribute to internalized standards that equate output with worth.

We operate on scripts that run silently in the background: If I stop, everything falls apart. My worth is tied to what I produce. If I don't do it, it will not get finished correctly. Being needed makes me valuable. According to self-determination theory, when basic psychological needs become tied to performance, individuals are more likely to develop externally driven motivation and persistent internal pressure (Ryan & Deci, 2017). As a result, when your body signals fatigue, your mind negotiates. Did we earn it yet? Meanwhile, your body is not negotiating. Your body is responding.

Closely connected to this is the association between productivity and identity. Completing tasks provides a sense of accomplishment and control, reinforced neurologically through dopamine release (Sapolsky, 2004). Over time, busyness begins to feel like purpose. However, when self-worth becomes contingent upon productivity, rest begins to feel like failure. And that is an unwinnable cycle, because if you stop, you are not always sure who you are without all the doing.

These beliefs are not your fault. They were taught, and what is learned can be unlearned. But first it has to be named.

The Weight You Carry

Relational dynamics further reinforce this pattern. Many high-achieving women occupy roles in which they are consistently relied upon. They are the problem-solvers, the organizers, the ones who figure it out. And because they are capable, others continue to depend on them. Research on role overload, a concept organizational psychologists have studied since the 1960s, demonstrates that individuals who carry excessive emotional and practical responsibilities experience higher levels of chronic stress and burnout (Kahn et al., 1964). Over time, being dependable becomes synonymous with being valuable. But dependence is not the same as reciprocity.

Because you are not just one person. You are a constellation of roles: the leader, the partner, the mother, the daughter, the friend, the mentor, the volunteer. Each role carries its own expectations, its own demands on your time, its own emotional weight. When you wear too many hats, your neck gets tired. The sheer volume of responsibilities is exactly the role overload just described, and it accumulates whether or not anyone acknowledges it.

The challenge is that each role feels important.

When Helping Becomes Self-Abandonment

There is a point in the cycle of overextension where helping shifts into something else. It moves from genuine care into a pattern of self-abandonment, where your own needs, wants, rest, and well-being become consistently last on the list, if they appear at all.

Let's define it plainly. Self-abandonment is the ongoing practice of deprioritizing your own needs, feelings, and limits in order to meet the needs of someone or something else, until you are no longer factored into your own life as a person who also requires care. It is not a single moment of sacrifice. It is a pattern, repeated so consistently that it starts to feel like your personality rather than what it actually is: a learned response to feeling safer when you are useful than when you are simply being.

And this is important: self-abandonment does not only show up in how you treat other people. It shows up anywhere you have extended past your capacity and kept going anyway. At work, it looks like saying yes to the extra project, the extra shift, the extra deadline, long after your body has already told you there is nothing left to give.

In your business, it looks like reinvesting every hour and every dollar back into growth while your own health, rest, and joy get treated as expenses you cannot yet afford. In parenting, it looks like showing up fully for every recital, every meal, every bedtime, while disappearing from your own list of people worth showing up for. In caregiving, whether for a parent, a partner, or an extended family member, it looks like becoming so fluent in everyone else's needs that you forget the shape of your own.

Self-abandonment does not always feel dramatic. It looks like skipping your own doctor's appointment to take someone else to theirs. It looks like postponing your personal goals to support everyone around you reaching theirs. It looks like saying "I'm fine" so many times that you stop checking in with yourself long enough to know whether you actually are.

You become everything for everyone except someone who is cared for.

Constantly being the source of support without receiving it in return contributes directly to emotional exhaustion. Somewhere in that exchange, you stopped being a recipient and became only a resource.

Here is where it gets complicated, because much of this gets carried under a name that sounds noble: sacrifice. I hear it often. I made a big sacrifice to take care of my mother. I sacrifice for my kids. I sacrifice for my team. And to be clear, sacrifice itself is not the problem. Choosing to give up something for the people and things you love is part of what love, parenting, and caregiving actually require. The distortion happens when sacrifice becomes the label we put on self-abandonment so it feels acceptable, even honorable, instead of what it actually is.

Research on sacrifice offers a useful distinction here. Studies on why people give things up for others have found that sacrifice motivated by genuinely wanting to nurture a relationship or care for someone you love is associated with better well-being, while sacrifice motivated by fear, guilt, or the need to avoid conflict or disapproval is associated with lower well-being and, over time, resentment (Impett et al., 2005).

In other words, the sacrifice itself is not what determines the cost. The why underneath it is. A sacrifice made from love can coexist with your well-being. When a sacrifice comes from fear, guilt, obligation, or the sense that you have no other choice, it stops being a gift. It becomes self-abandonment wearing sacrifice's name.

This is why so many caregivers describe the same contradiction: I would do it again, and I am exhausted and a little resentful that I had to. Both things can be true. Caring for a parent, raising children, showing up for the people you love: these are not signs that something is wrong with you. But sacrifice without boundaries stops being sustainable, and it stops being fully yours to give. It is not selfish to protect pieces of your time, your health, and your identity while you are caring for someone else. It is what allows the sacrifice to remain a gift instead of becoming the thing that costs you yourself.

The People-Pleasing Trap

People-pleasing is often disguised as kindness, flexibility, and being easy to work with. And sometimes it is those things. But for many women, people-pleasing runs much deeper than agreeableness. It is rooted in fear: the difficulty saying no, the fear of disappointing others, the deep and persistent need for approval.

You avoid conflict at the cost of your own peace. You take on over-responsibility for how others feel, walking on eggshells to ensure everyone else is comfortable while you are quietly suffocating beneath the weight of it. You say yes in the meeting and feel resentful on the drive home. You volunteer for the thing nobody wanted because you could not bear the discomfort of being the one who did not.

You keep saying you are tired, but you keep volunteering for exhaustion.

As discussed earlier in this chapter, people-pleasing is frequently a manifestation of the fawn trauma response, a survival mechanism developed from prolonged exposure to environments where your safety or worth felt conditional (Walker, 2013). You learned that the best way to stay safe was to keep everyone else happy. This is also where hyper-independence is born, the belief that you must do it all yourself so you will not burden anyone or risk rejection. On the outside, it looks like strength and self-sufficiency. On the inside, it is a trauma response wearing a very convincing cape.

This is the same appeasement response introduced earlier: when fight, flight, and freeze do not feel safe or available, the nervous system defaults to keeping the peace. What begins as protection becomes, over time, personality. And you stop being able to tell the difference between who you genuinely are and who you have learned you need to be in order to be safe.

Resentment as a Warning Sign

Here is something I want you to hold: resentment is not a character flaw. Resentment is a signal. It is the emotional alarm that sounds when you have been giving more than you have been receiving for too long. When you have been saying yes on the outside while screaming no on the inside. When you have been helping everyone else while

going without.

If you find yourself feeling irritable, bitter, or quietly resentful toward the people and responsibilities that used to feel meaningful, pay attention. That feeling is not ingratitude. It is depletion trying to get your attention in the only language available to it.

Later in this book, we will explore how boundaries, capacity awareness, and intentional limits help interrupt these patterns. For now, simply notice where your desire to help may be costing you more than you realized. The awareness itself matters, because you cannot begin to change what you have not yet been willing to see.

What This Sounds Like From the Inside

Three moments come up again and again in my work. See whether any of them sound like your own voice.

1. **Anxious on vacation.** The thought underneath is, if I am not working, I am falling behind. Rest that does not restore is not rest. You brought the ledger with you.
2. **Waking early to get ahead.** The thought underneath is, my value is measured by how much I accomplish before other people even start. The day begins already overdrawn.
3. **No day off, and guilty anyway.** The thought underneath is, I have not done enough to stop yet. When stopping has to be justified, capacity can never be protected. It can only be spent.

I worked with a senior attorney who grew up in a house where the only reliable praise came from excelling. Home was unpredictable. Achievement was not. Success became the one thing that made her feel safe, so slowing down did not register as rest. It registered as danger.

When slowing down feels dangerous, you will override your capacity every time, and you will call it drive.

If any of that sounded familiar, here is something to put up against it.

Something to Say to Yourself

I am not only valuable when I am producing.

My worth is inherent, not earned.

I am allowed to live fully, not just function.

Rest is part of that life, not a reward for finishing it.

Hustle Culture

Somewhere along the way, we got the message that success and suffering go together. We normalized being tired, glorified being busy, celebrated the grind, stress bragged about how little we sleep and how much we carry, and felt guilty for resting. And then we wondered why we were drained. We were never taught how to succeed without abandoning ourselves.

Let me be clear. Hustle is not the enemy. Unhealthy hustle is. You can be well and be ambitious. You can build your life and protect your peace. You can pursue more without losing yourself in the process. That is what this book is here to help you do.

Hustle culture did not emerge out of nowhere. It grew from the entrepreneurial and startup boom of the early 2000s, when innovation and relentless ambition became the defining values of success. The rise of social media turned productivity into a performance. Entrepreneurs began sharing curated highlight reels, the launch days, the revenue screenshots, the five a.m. routines, without showing the anxiety, the loneliness, or the depletion behind the scenes.

The message became inescapable: you need multiple income streams, you need constant content creation to remain relevant, you need to be building, growing, and optimizing every waking hour. And if you are not, somewhere, someone else is, and they are getting ahead while you rest.

This environment also breeds what has come to be called "stress bragging," the practice of complaining about busyness while implicitly seeking validation for one's dedication. Research on busyness as a modern status symbol confirms the shift: being exhausted became a status symbol, and being overwhelmed became a badge of commitment (Bellezza et al., 2017). And somewhere in that shift, rest became something to be ashamed of.

Comparison culture does the rest. When your feed is full of other people's best moments, it is almost impossible not to measure your behind-the-scenes against their highlights. That comparison does not inspire. It depletes. And it keeps you running, not toward your own vision, but away from the fear of being left behind.

Activity vs. Progress

One of the sneakiest symptoms of hustle culture is the confusion between activity and actual forward movement. You are busy. You are always busy. But busy is not the same as strategic, and motion is not the same as momentum.

Hustle culture encourages a lack of focus and a constant chasing of trends. You pivot when the algorithm shifts. You rebrand when someone else's launch looks more polished than yours. You start over again because the current strategy is not producing fast enough results. And the exhaustion mounts not because you are not capable, but because you are constantly beginning without ever building.

You can be incredibly busy and completely stagnant.

Exhaustion is not a measure of success.

There is a version of ambition that is life-giving. It is rooted in clarity about what you are building and why. It is connected to your values, sustained by genuine passion, and it makes room for rest because it understands that you are the engine, and engines require fuel.

And then there is the version that hustle culture produces. Frantic. Comparison-driven. Fueled by the fear of falling behind rather than the joy of moving forward. This version cannot rest because rest is where the fear gets loud. Rest is where the questions come: Is this enough? Am I enough? What if I fall behind?

That is not ambition. That is anxiety with a vision board.

Wellness and ambition are not opposites. But you have to be willing to believe that before the grind will loosen its grip.

The Productivity Trap

This pattern is not just personal. It is structural. The traditional nine-to-five model was designed for output, not well-being, and even when organizations offer time off, it is often tied to approval processes that create stress before you have begun to recover. Deadlines do not shift because you are overwhelmed. Expectations do not adjust because you are exhausted. Over time, you learn to silence your needs to meet external demands.

For many women, this shows up most concretely in the size of their caseload. Whether you are a social worker, a nurse, a teacher, a case manager, or anyone whose job is measured in how many people you are responsible for, the number keeps climbing while the hours in the day do not. When the caseload exceeds what is humanly manageable, something has to give, and too often what gives is quality, thoroughness, or your own well-being.

You start cutting corners you never intended to cut, not because you do not care, but because there is no version of doing it all the right way in the time you have been given. That gap between the standard you were trained to meet and the capacity you actually have is its own quiet source of shame, and it is rarely named as a systems failure. It is felt as a personal one.

Turnover and layoffs make this worse. When a colleague leaves, or a position is eliminated, the work they were doing does not disappear. It gets redistributed, and often without discussion, to the people who are still there. Your job description stays the same on paper while what you are actually expected to carry keeps expanding. When you ask about it, you are often told that you are simply responsible for "additional duties as assigned," that small, unremarkable line near the bottom of the job description that somehow ends up justifying almost anything.

And because you are dependable, because you are the one who figures it out, you absorb it. You are still expected to be a team player, to keep morale up, to not complain, even while you are doing the work of two or three people and watching your own capacity get further and further exceeded.

There is also a quieter dynamic at play here, one that rarely gets named. When you are seen as competent, people do not just rely on you. They expect more of you. Your skill becomes the justification for the extra load, not a reason to protect your time. Colleagues and leadership alike lean on the person who can be counted on to figure it out, and that reliability, without a corresponding increase in pay, title, or support, starts to look less like recognition and more like exploitation.

Being good at your job should not become the reason more and more gets added to your plate. Competence may increase what people expect from you, but it does not mean you have more capacity to carry it. Research on healthcare teams confirms what this feels like from the inside: employees on understaffed teams with frequent turnover and workloads that exceed capacity are significantly more likely to experience burnout than those on fully staffed, stable teams (Helfrich et al., 2017). Understaffing is not a personal shortfall. It is a measurable risk factor, and your body is not wrong for responding to it as one.

This creates what can be understood as the productivity trap, a cycle in which your value becomes tied to how much you can produce, how much you can carry, and how consistently you can perform. The more you do, the more is expected. The more you give, the more is required. And eventually, you begin to lose sight of where you end and your responsibilities begin.

The roles you carry, the hats you wear, and the busyness you have learned to treat as proof of your worth did not appear by accident. They were built, reinforced, and rewarded, one yes at a time, until you stopped noticing how much of it was ever really yours. That noticing is not to be ignored. It is information. It is the beginning of choosing differently.

Hard Truth

You keep trying to get better at carrying the weight of your responsibilities. The truth is, you were never meant to carry all of it alone.

Chapter Summary

Renata was not disorganized, and she was not doing too little. She was absorbing the invisible labor of every room she walked into, and no structure around her was built to notice.

1. **The pattern does not live in you alone.** It is held in place by workplaces, roles, and a culture that all reward the same overextension.
2. **The systems around you were built for output, not well-being.** Rest is treated as something to be approved rather than something you need.
3. **Much of what you carry is invisible.** The mental load, the emotional labor, the remembering, appears on no spreadsheet and shows up in no paycheck, but it spends real capacity.
4. **Sacrifice and self-abandonment are not the same thing.** Sacrifice made from love can coexist with your well-being. Sacrifice made from fear, guilt, or fear of disappointing others quietly erases you.
5. **Hustle culture calls your depletion ambition**. It profits from your belief that rest is a reward and busyness is proof of worth.
6. **Capacity is what none of it accounts for.** Every system in this chapter assumes your limits are negotiable. They are not.

CAPACITY CHECK

Name What You're Carrying

Take a moment to sit with what came up for you in this chapter. Not to fix it. Not to overanalyze it. Just to notice it.

On the Systems and Beliefs That Keep Me Stuck

1. What belief keeps me pushing even when I feel exhausted, and where did I first learn it?
2. Where in my life am I calling something a sacrifice when it has quietly become self-abandonment?

3. Which of my roles, at work, in my business, as a parent, or as a caregiver, has taken more than I currently have left to give?
4. Do I notice resentment building anywhere in my life right now? What might it be trying to tell me?
5. Where am I wearing exhaustion or busyness like a badge instead of naming it as a problem to address?

Chapter 5

It Was Never Just You

Toxic Systems, Entrepreneurship, and Helping Professions

"You either walk inside your story and own it
or you stand outside your story and hustle for your worthiness."
~ Brené Brown

Monica was the one everyone called first.

If the church needed someone to run the women's ministry, Monica said yes. If her business needed a website updated at eleven at night because a client was launching in the morning, Monica stayed up and updated it. If her sister needed a ride, her mother needed a favor, her team at work needed someone to stay late and fix what leadership had broken, Monica was already reaching for her keys before anyone finished asking.

She built her consulting business from nothing, one client at a time, answering emails from her phone in parking lots between meetings. She led a team of nine at her day job, the job that paid the bills while the business grew. She sat on the leadership board at her church, where she was known, affectionately, as the one who "just gets it done." She was somebody's daughter, somebody's auntie, somebody's go-to friend for the 2 a.m. phone call. Every room she walked into had already decided what she was there to carry.

Nobody ever sat Monica down and asked her how she was holding up. They asked what time she'd have the deck ready. They asked if she could cover the second service. They asked if she had a minute, and she always did, because that was the role, and she had played it so long she no longer remembered auditioning for it.

There was a Tuesday when Monica sat on the bottom step of her own staircase, keys still in her hand, and could not make herself get up. Nothing had happened. That was the strange part. No crisis, no confrontation, nothing she could point to and say, this is why. Just the accumulated weight of being dependable in every direction at once, with no direction pointed back toward her.

Somewhere beneath all those expectations, beneath the deck that was always ready and the second service that was always covered and the 2 a.m. phone calls she always answered, Monica disappeared. Not all at once. A little at a time, in every room that needed her to be the strong one, until there was no room left where she got to simply be.

Chapter 3 asked you to look inward, at the beliefs, the wounds, and the roles that keep you pushing past what is sustainable. This chapter asks you to look around. Because some of what you have been carrying was never only about what is happening inside you. Some of it is about where you are standing when it happens: the workplace that runs on fear instead of trust, the business you built with your own hands and no one to hand anything off to, the profession that asks you to keep giving long after your shift ends, the leadership seat that came with influence but not with a single person checking on you, the ministry that told you rest was something you had not yet earned.

Naming your patterns matters. That was Chapter 3's work. But your patterns do not exist in a vacuum, and neither do you. Monica was not lacking discipline or willpower. She was operating inside four systems at once, each one asking for a full version of her and none of them asking what she had left to give. Every one of those rooms does the same thing in a different accent. It asks for more than you have, and it rarely asks what you have. Understanding these systems will not fix them overnight. But it will help you stop asking what is wrong with you when the truth was never that simple. This chapter is about the rooms themselves, and about the one thread that runs quietly beneath every one of them: capacity.

Part I: The Systems That Drain Us

Toxic Work Environments

Not every workplace challenge is about how much you have on your plate. Sometimes it is about the environment in which you are carrying all of it. A toxic work environment does not just add to your stress. It fundamentally changes how your nervous system functions at work, and over time, everywhere else. It does not just ask more of you than is reasonable. It exceeds your capacity by design, then calls the excess your job description.

Toxic workplaces are not always obvious. They do not always involve overt hostility or dramatic confrontation. Sometimes toxicity is subtle, embedded in the culture, and normalized to the point where you stop questioning the environment and start questioning yourself instead.

The signs are worth naming clearly: micromanagement that communicates distrust, favoritism that creates a tiered sense of belonging, poor leadership that models dysfunction and calls it strength, a lack of transparency that keeps people anxious and uninformed, high turnover that tells you, if you are paying attention, exactly how people feel about staying, workplace gossip that erodes trust, and fear-based leadership that demands compliance over collaboration.

According to a report from MIT Sloan Management Review, toxic workplace culture is more than ten times more likely to contribute to an employee leaving their job than low pay. It was also identified as the primary reason people left their jobs during the Great Resignation (Sull et al., 2022). People were not leaving for more money. They were leaving to breathe.

Psychological Safety and the Nervous System

Amy Edmondson defines psychological safety as a shared belief that a team is safe for interpersonal risk-taking, that individuals can speak up, ask questions, and admit mistakes without fear of negative consequences (Edmondson, 1999). When psychological safety is absent, employees operate in a state of hypervigilance. You are constantly monitoring your environment for threats, trying to anticipate the next unreasonable demand or unwarranted criticism. This is not a character trait. This is a nervous system under sustained threat.

When psychological safety is low, the cost shows up in exactly the ways this book has been describing. In environments where individuals do not feel safe being honest about their capacity, their concerns, or their struggles, they are far more likely to overperform in silence rather than ask for relief, and that silence has been linked to the emotional exhaustion at the heart of burnout.

This is not just a workplace theory. Psychiatrist Sandra Bloom built an entire model around it. In the early 1980s, working in Philadelphia, Bloom developed what became known as the Sanctuary Model, a trauma-informed approach to organizational change grounded in a simple but powerful observation: organizations can carry trauma the same way individuals do (S. L. Bloom, 2017). Just as a person who has been through prolonged stress or harm can become hypervigilant, isolated, or reactive, an organization under chronic pressure can develop those same patterns, showing up as poor communication, rigid hierarchy, and a culture where people stop feeling safe enough to speak honestly. Bloom called this the parallel process, and it named something many of us have felt inside dysfunctional workplaces without ever having language for it.

The Sanctuary Model was built to interrupt that cycle by making psychological, and moral, safety a structural priority rather than an aspiration. It asks organizations to commit to nonviolence, emotional intelligence, open communication, and shared decision-making as concrete practices, not values posted on a break room wall. Between 2005 and 2016, more than 350 social service, mental health, and juvenile justice organizations were trained in this model, beginning with a citywide effort here in Philadelphia and eventually reaching programs across the country and internationally (Bloom et al., 2007; Yanosy et al., 2015). The premise still holds wherever it lands: you cannot build psychological safety for the people an organization serves while the people doing the serving are operating in an unsafe, unsupported environment. Safety has to be built into the system, not left to the willpower of the people inside it.

What Toxicity Costs You

The mental health consequences of sustained exposure to a toxic environment are significant and well-documented. Research indicates that working in an environment with a poor psychosocial safety climate can triple the risk of developing new depression symptoms (Zadow et al., 2021). Chronic anxiety, hypervigilance, and compassion fatigue are common responses to fear-based, unpredictable workplaces. When you never know where you stand, when leadership is inconsistent, or when your performance is evaluated through a lens of bias rather than equity, your nervous system stays on alert.

You are not just doing your job. You are also constantly assessing threats. And that dual labor, the work itself plus the ongoing vigilance required to survive the environment, is exhausting in a way that a better morning routine will not fix.

Burnout in toxic environments does not just affect how you feel. It affects how you function. You show up. You go through the motions. But the part of you that used to do this work with energy and purpose has gone somewhere to recover.

In toxic environments, employees who are known for stepping in often end up carrying more than their share. When leadership is poor or inconsistent, dependable people can become the ones who fill the gaps, take on what has been left unattended, and keep things moving when the system is struggling. But just because you are capable of carrying more does not mean more should be placed on you. Your competence should not be mistaken for unlimited capacity. Over time, constantly compensating for problems you did not create can leave you depleted.

The cost of a toxic environment is rarely limited to how you feel about your job. It registers in three places at once, and the third one is the one people notice last.

What It Costs You at Work	How It Shows Up	What It Does to the Work Itself
Anxiety	Constant dread of what comes next, and difficulty focusing while on alert	Reduced concentration, because it is hard to focus when your nervous system is scanning for danger
Depression	A tripled risk in workplaces with a poor psychosocial safety climate	Decreased productivity, as output drops even while hours increase
Hypervigilance	Always scanning for the next threat	Presenteeism, meaning physically there and mentally gone
Compassion fatigue	Emotional depletion from sustained care	Disengagement, because caring has started to hurt
Reduced emotional intelligence	Self-regulation, empathy, and your read on other people all decline under chronic stress	Absenteeism, when calling in sick becomes a survival strategy rather than an excuse

The Residue of a Toxic Workplace Doesn't Stay At Work

What It Costs You Beyond Work	How It Shows Up
Relationship strain	The stress follows you home and into your family
Emotional withdrawal	Nothing left to give the people you love

Loss of identity	You forget who you are outside of survival mode
Physical toll	Chronic stress settles in the body as sleep loss, headaches, and a weakened immune system

In fear-based environments, communication breaks down. People stop sharing ideas, stop asking questions, and stop collaborating, not because they have nothing to contribute, but because contributing feels risky. The focus shifts from doing good work to avoiding blame. Silos form not out of indifference but out of self-protection. And in those silos, burnout compounds.

A toxic work environment does not clock out when you do. The stress follows you home. It strains your relationships, shortens your patience with the people you love, and robs you of the ability to be fully present in the spaces that are supposed to restore you. You are physically there, but emotionally depleted. You are engaged, but stretched thin. At some point, the question shifts from "Can I handle this?" to "At what cost am I handling this?" That question matters. The cost is real. And it is personal.

When the Business Becomes the Burnout

Toxic systems are not confined to traditional employment. They show up, often in more intense ways, for the woman who thought building her own business would finally put her back in control of her time. For individuals who are self-employed, productivity is directly tied to livelihood. The more you work, the more you can earn. The more you create, the more opportunities you generate. On the surface, this appears empowering. In practice, it can exceed the same capacity a toxic job would have exceeded, just with your name on the letterhead instead of someone else's.

When your income depends on your effort, slowing down does not feel like a choice. It feels like risk. Taking a sick day means lost revenue. Rest means falling behind. And so the grind continues, not from ambition, but from necessity. Research reflects the intensity of this experience: in one widely cited study, nearly half of entrepreneurs reported a personal history of a mental health condition such as depression, ADHD, or anxiety, and 72% were affected either directly or through immediate family (Freeman et al., 2019). Entrepreneurs are also more likely than the general population to experience depression and emotional exhaustion due to financial uncertainty, role overload, and the ongoing pressure to sustain and grow their businesses. Constant output without structure is not sustainability. It is survival. And survival, over time, leads to exhaustion.

Many entrepreneurs, particularly solopreneurs in the early stages, spend the majority of their time working in their business rather than on their business. They are operating simultaneously as the strategist, the marketer, the accountant, the customer service representative, the content creator, and the service provider, wearing all the hats and providing the service, and the load is invisible to everyone who only sees the finished product.

Without adequate infrastructure, support systems, or financial capacity to delegate, the responsibility becomes all-encompassing. And the cycle it produces is unsustainable: high effort, low clarity, constant reaction, and the creeping feeling that no matter how hard you work, you are not making the kind of progress that justifies what it is costing you. For business owners managing teams, the pressure evolves rather than disappears. Leadership adds the demand of managing people, navigating interpersonal dynamics, addressing operational challenges, and holding the emotional ecosystem of everyone involved. You are not just running a business. You are holding the energy of everyone in it.

There is a particular kind of exhaustion that belongs to the woman running more than one business at a time. Maybe it is a full brand and a consulting arm. Maybe it is a boutique, a coaching practice, and a product line she launched during a season when she had more energy than she does now. She did not set out to overextend herself. Each venture made sense on its own. Together, they have become more than one person can carry.

The serial entrepreneur often does not have a team behind any of it. She is not choosing which business to give her best to. She is dividing herself, unevenly and often invisibly, among all of them, and still trying to show up fully for each one. One brand gets the marketing this week. Another gets whatever energy is left over. A third quietly stalls, not from lack of vision, but from lack of capacity. Nothing is failing. Nothing is thriving either. Everything is simply surviving on whatever she has left to give it.

This is where ambition and capacity have to be told apart. Having the vision to build multiple streams of income is not the problem. Believing you must personally execute all of it, without a team, without systems, without boundaries between one venture and the next, is what turns vision into depletion. You can hold big dreams and still need help carrying them. Wanting to build more does not mean you were built to do it all alone.

Social media has added a layer of pressure to entrepreneurship that did not exist for previous generations of business owners. In the current landscape, visibility often feels synonymous with viability. If you are not posting consistently, you are not growing. If you are not showing up online, you are falling behind. And so the content treadmill begins. Content creation fatigue is real. The demand to perform your business publicly, to brand your personal life, and to project momentum regardless of what is actually happening behind the scenes creates a kind of performance exhaustion that is separate from, and layered on top of, the actual work of building a business. You are constantly learning without implementing, constantly creating without resting, and constantly comparing your behind-the-scenes to someone else's highlight reel.

The financial dimension of entrepreneurship creates a category of stress that is distinct from traditional employment. There is no guaranteed paycheck. Benefits are not tied to a steady salary. And when there is no separation between your income and your effort, the stakes of slowing down feel existential. Financial pressure can become one of the most powerful drivers of burnout because it attaches a survival narrative to productivity. When working more literally means eating, paying rent, covering your team, sustaining your family, the idea of resting feels irresponsible rather than necessary. And from that place, hustle is not a culture. It is a coping mechanism.

The challenge is often not a lack of ambition. It is a lack of clarity and structure. Many entrepreneurs are learning as they go, navigating business development through trial and error, without the systems that make sustainability possible: financial tracking, defined workflows, standard operating procedures. Without that infrastructure, time and energy are spent reacting rather than building. You are working more, but not necessarily moving forward in the way you intended. The shift begins not with doing more, but with doing differently. It involves building systems, creating boundaries, and developing strategies that support both growth and well-being.

A business that depends on your constant depletion is not a business model. It is a burnout cycle. And the ripple effect extends beyond revenue. It affects your work, your relationships, your patience, and your presence. At some point, you have to ask not just whether the business is growing, but whether you are surviving it. Sustainable success is possible. But it requires a willingness to build differently than hustle culture taught you to. It requires you to be well enough to lead well. And that begins with telling the truth about what this is actually costing you.

Helping Professions: When Caring Becomes Carrying

There is another category of exhaustion this chapter would be incomplete without, and it belongs to the women whose entire job description is other people. Not because these professions are simply hard, plenty of jobs are hard, but because they require you to spend a resource that does not show up on a schedule: your emotional capacity, hour after hour, person after person, often with no built-in time to refill it.

Educators

Teaching requires far more than delivering lessons. Teachers are educators, mentors, counselors, mediators, crisis responders, encouragers, and emotional anchors for dozens, sometimes hundreds, of students each week. Long after the dismissal bell rings, many continue grading papers, preparing lessons, responding to parents, attending meetings, worrying about struggling students, and planning for tomorrow.

The issue is rarely that teachers lack passion. Many simply continue working long after their emotional, cognitive, and physical capacity has been exceeded. National workforce data bears this out: RAND's State of the American Teacher surveys have found teachers reporting frequent job-related stress at about twice the rate of the general population of working adults (Steiner et al., 2022), and Gallup polling has found that K-12 workers report the highest burnout rate of any industry in the country (Marken & Agrawal, 2022). Skaalvik and Skaalvik's research on teacher emotional exhaustion points to the same root: it is not any single classroom variable so much as the relentless time pressure and the ongoing demand to regulate your own emotions while managing everyone else's (Skaalvik & Skaalvik, 2017). When educational systems consistently require more than one person can sustainably give, burnout becomes a predictable outcome rather than a personal failure.

Healthcare Professionals

Healthcare professionals spend their days caring for people during some of the most vulnerable moments of their lives. Whether working in hospitals, primary care, rehabilitation, hospice, or emergency medicine, they are expected to remain emotionally regulated, make difficult decisions, respond quickly, and continue providing compassionate care despite carrying their own stress and fatigue. The National Academy of Medicine has named clinician burnout a system-level patient safety issue rather than an individual shortcoming, and research from Shanafelt and colleagues has tracked physician burnout and declining satisfaction with work-life integration across more than a decade of national surveys, with distress rising sharply under the added strain of recent years (Shanafelt et al., 2022).

Many become so focused on caring for others that they unintentionally neglect their own well-being. Compassion should never require self-abandonment. The ability to continue caring for others depends upon protecting the capacity to care for yourself.

Therapists and Social Workers

As a therapist myself, I understand this one personally. People often assume that because therapists understand mental health, they are somehow protected from burnout. The opposite is often true. Every session requires presence. Every difficult story requires emotional regulation. Every crisis requires steadiness. Maslach and Leiter, whose framework has shaped decades of burnout research, describe burnout as a response to chronic, unrelieved job stress characterized by exhaustion, cynicism, and a diminished sense of accomplishment, and few professions absorb chronic stress as directly, session after session, as this one does (Maslach & Leiter, 2022).

Social workers often carry additional responsibilities, including high caseloads, documentation demands, crisis intervention, advocacy, limited community resources, and the emotional weight of helping people navigate broken systems. Researchers have given specific names to the toll this takes: Bride's work on secondary traumatic stress describes the way absorbing other people's trauma, again and again, can begin to mirror trauma symptoms in the helper (Bride, 2007), and Newell and MacNeil's research on compassion fatigue describes the gradual erosion that happens when the well of empathy is drawn from constantly and rarely replenished (Newell & MacNeil, 2010).

Holding hope for others is meaningful work. It is also emotionally expensive work. When we continually pour into others without replenishing ourselves, our own capacity eventually begins to diminish.

Nonprofit and Community Workers

Many nonprofit professionals entered this work because they genuinely wanted to make a difference. Purpose fuels their work. But purpose alone cannot protect someone from burnout. Limited funding, staff shortages, secondary trauma, compassion fatigue, increasing community needs, and the constant pressure to do more with less often create environments where people continually operate beyond their capacity. Chronic understaffing and underfunding do not just strain a budget. They strain the people asked to make up the difference, and burnout research has long identified that mismatch between what a job demands and the resources available to meet it as one of burnout's most reliable drivers (Maslach & Leiter, 2016).

Passion may explain why someone enters the work. Capacity determines how long they can sustainably remain in it.

No matter the profession, one truth remains. Burnout is rarely evidence of weakness. More often, it is evidence that the demands placed upon you have consistently exceeded the capacity available to carry them. That is not simply an individual issue. It is also a systems issue.

But underneath all of it is a truth this chapter has been circling from the start. This was never really about occupations. It is about identity. The common thread connecting these rooms is not the job title. It is the woman standing in the middle of them.

Whether she is a teacher, a therapist, a nurse, a nonprofit director, an entrepreneur, or all of the above in a single week, she has often quietly become the dependable one. The responsible one. The helper. The fixer. The one who is called first because everyone has learned, correctly, that she will say yes.

Without ever deciding to, she has begun measuring her worth by how much she can carry, and the rooms she serves have learned to count on that measurement too. This chapter is not only trying to describe burnout. It is trying to help you understand why so many high-capacity women eventually run empty, and why running empty was never a character flaw.

Chapter Summary

Monica was not undisciplined, and she was not disorganized. She was standing inside several systems at once, each one asking for a full version of her, and not one of them asking what she had left.

1. **It was never only about you.** The patterns you named earlier are real, but they do not happen in a vacuum. Where you are standing shapes what it costs you to stand there.

2. **A toxic environment is not just stressful.** It is a nervous system under sustained threat. When psychological safety is missing, you are doing your job and assessing for danger at the same time. That dual labor is exhausting in a way no morning routine will fix.

3. **Owning the business does not remove the system.** It can relocate it. When your income depends entirely on your effort, rest stops feeling like a choice and starts feeling like a risk.

4. **Helping professions spend a resource that is not on the schedule.** Teaching, healthcare, therapy, social work, and community work all run on emotional capacity, hour after hour, usually with no built-in time to refill it.

5. **The rooms rarely ask what you have.** Every environment in this chapter asks for more than you have and almost never asks what you have. That is the thread running underneath all of them.

6. **Understanding the system is not the same as excusing it.** You may not be able to change every room overnight. You can stop asking what is wrong with you when the answer was never that simple.

The system was never built to notice what it was costing you.

Hard Truth

> You keep asking what is wrong with you.
> When will you ask what is wrong with the room?

CAPACITY CHECK

Consider Your Environment

Take a moment to sit with what came up for you in this chapter and pay attention to your body's response. What do you physically feel? What do you emotionally feel? What were your thoughts?

This is information to pay attention to.

1. Do I feel safe enough, psychologically, to be honest about my capacity where I work or serve?

2. Have I quietly absorbed additional duties, a bigger caseload, or someone else's workload without ever renegotiating what is reasonable?

3. If I am a business owner, am I spread across more ventures or responsibilities than I can currently sustain? Does my business depend on my constant depletion to keep running, or could it survive me stepping back?

4. If my work centers on caring for others, do I have anything in place that replenishes the same capacity my job asks me to spend?

5. Which of the rooms in this chapter: work, business, or a helping profession is currently asking more of me than I have to give?

Chapter 6

The Isolation of Leadership and Serving

Leadership and Ministry, the Two Roles That Isolate

"Let us not grow weary in doing good,
for in due season we will reap, if we do not give up."
~ Galatians 6:9

Pastor Yvonne could fill a room with her presence and empty herself doing it. On Sunday she stood before a congregation that loved her, and by Monday afternoon she was answering a member's crisis call in a grocery store parking lot, the ice cream melting in the trunk while she prayed someone through the worst day of their life. She led a ministry that a few corners of her own denomination still would not fully recognize, because their doctrine did not make room for a woman in her role. So she carried that too, the quiet work of proving she belonged in a seat she had been called to but not always welcomed into.

During the week, she managed a team of fourteen at her day job. There, the isolation wore a different outfit. She could not tell her supervisor she was drowning, because drowning looked like incompetence, and she had worked too hard to be seen that way. She could not tell her team either, because she needed their respect more than she needed their sympathy, and transparency, she had learned, could cost her both. So she stood in the middle, holding the pressure from above and the needs from below, with no one beside her.

And then there was home, the part no one saw at all. Her marriage was straining in ways she had not said out loud to a single person. She believed in her vows, believed God could hold what was breaking, and so she stayed and prayed and tried, quietly, to keep it together. But the shame of it kept her silent.

What would it look like, the woman who counseled other people's marriages, admitting her own was cracking? So, she said nothing. She smiled on Sunday, led on Monday, and came home to a house where the presentation of a perfect life grew heavier every day it stayed a presentation.

Everyone in Yvonne's life had somewhere to bring their burdens. Her staff had her. Her congregation had her. Her family had her. Yvonne had a locked car, a melting carton of ice cream, a marriage she was holding together with faith and silence, and a God she trusted but was still learning to rest in. She was surrounded by people, all day, every day. And she was profoundly alone.

So far, this book has looked at the systems and professions that quietly exceed our capacity. But there are two roles that deserve their own attention, because the exhaustion they produce is compounded by something specific: isolation. Women in leadership and women in ministry are often surrounded by people and profoundly alone in their struggle at the same time. Both are expected to hold everyone else's burdens. Neither is given many places to set their own down. Like Yvonne, both are trusted precisely because they never seem to run out, until they do.

Women in Leadership: The Weight of Leading Without an Ally

Leadership looks like influence from the outside. From the inside, for many women, it often feels like isolation. You are the one people come to when something is wrong. You are rarely the one anyone checks on. The higher you rise, the fewer people feel safe enough to be honest with you, and the fewer people you feel safe enough to be honest with in return.

This is not a personal failing. It is a structural reality of leadership, and it hits women differently. Research from LeanIn.Org and McKinsey's Women in the Workplace study (2022) found that 43% of women leaders report being burned out, compared with 31% of men at their level. Women in leadership are not imagining the weight. They are carrying more of it, more often, with fewer people to share it with.

Part of this is structural. Women continue to be underrepresented at senior levels, which means fewer peers who share the vantage point of the role. Part of it is relational. Reporting on workplace loneliness points to a pattern in which women's isolation deepens rather than eases as they advance, often because mentorship, sponsorship, and informal support networks quietly thin out the higher they climb (Mikhail, 2024). And part of it is simply the nature of the seat. A leader cannot always say what she is thinking out loud to her team. It may unsettle them, or her supervisor, because it may look like she cannot handle the role. So, she holds it. Alone.

I know this one from the inside. For a long stretch of my own leadership, it was a lonely place. I did not have an ally, no one I could go to and simply say, I am overwhelmed. I did not fully trust that I could take that to the people above me, because I did not want to be seen as incapable of the role. But I could not take it to my team either, because being too open, too familiar, felt like it might cost me their respect. So, I learned to manage the stress of the middle by myself, holding the pressure from above and the needs from below, performing steadiness I did not always feel. It was a delicate dance, and most days I danced it alone.

This is where mentorship and true allyship become more than a nice addition to leadership development. They become protective. A leader without a confidant, without a peer who understands the specific weight of the seat she is in, is a leader who is absorbing everyone else's stress with nowhere to put her own. That kind of isolation does not just affect the leader. It affects the whole team, because a depleted leader eventually leads from depletion.

Workplace research has long confirmed the ripple effect: people rarely leave companies; they leave leadership, and the relationship with one's direct supervisor shapes the decision to stay or go more than pay or the work itself (Gallup, Inc., 2015).

This places a responsibility on leaders that many were never equipped for, particularly women who were promoted for their competence and work ethic rather than trained in people leadership. Nobody sat them down and asked how they lead, only whether they could deliver. That gap does not make someone a bad leader. It does make it harder to lead well, and harder still to recognize when your own unresolved stress is shaping how your team experiences you.

If this is you, here is the reframe: developing self-awareness about how you lead is not an indictment of your capability. It is an act of care, for your team and for yourself. You cannot pour clarity, patience, or direction into other people from a nervous system that is running on empty. The leader who is well enough to reflect on her own patterns is the leader who can actually build the kind of environment people do not want to leave.

There is one more thing this kind of isolation asks of you, and it deserves to be named plainly, because it quietly costs the most. When everyone depends on you, you learn to wear a mask. You show up strong. You show up put together. You present as though you have the answers, because the people around you are expecting exactly that. This is true when working a nine-to-five, and it is true in ministry. A pastor, a first lady, a ministry leader, all of them walk into rooms where people expect them to know it all, to have it all handled, to embody a kind of certainty the rest of us are allowed to live without.

And here is the quiet trap. We are imperfect by nature. We may even say out loud that we are imperfect. But people still expect us to perform as though we are not. Leadership spaces, whether in a business or a house of worship, can be unforgiving and quick to judge, and that judgment takes a real toll on the mental and emotional capacity of the person carrying the role.

It creates a nagging, often unspoken pressure to do more, to prove you are as knowledgeable as everyone assumes you are. You may have several departments under you, supervisors and staff and workers who all report to you, and they are still turning to you for the answer. It is the same in ministry. The pastor and church leaders of the house are still expected to have it all, by the congregation, ministries, and by everyone who looks to them to hold it together. But we do not always have it. Nobody knows it all. Nobody is perfect. But the performance of knowing everything is exhausting, and it burns through you in a way no one around you can see.

What I have seen is that when leaders let themselves be human, when they are honest about their own limits, something shifts. It builds a kind of trust and relatability that performance never could. People do not connect with a flawless image. They connect with a real person.

I say this with love, because this comes out of my own life in the church. There is a real pressure on leaders to appear as though they have it all together, and I understand where it comes from. But I am deeply grateful for the leaders I have known who chose honesty instead, who were willing to be vulnerable and transparent about their own lives. That kind of openness did not make them smaller in my eyes. It made them people I could actually trust.

This is close to what Brené Brown's research on vulnerability has shown: the willingness to be seen, imperfections and all, is not a weakness in leadership but a source of connection and trust (Brown, 2012). But too often, people in these positions get put on a pedestal, and the pedestal comes with a cost. Now there is an image to uphold, and keeping up that image can quietly start to matter more than being honest about how you are really doing. The pressure only grows, because maintaining the role of the perfect leader, or the perfect person in ministry, becomes a full-time job on top of the one they already have.

That kind of sustained pressure does not stay contained. Over time, it can push a person straight into overwhelm and burnout, and burnout has a way of changing how you relate to people. In the research, one of the core features of burnout is exactly this: a growing cynicism and emotional distance from the very people you are there to serve (Maslach & Leiter, 2016). It is not that the leader stops caring. It is that there is nothing left to care with. On top of it is the constant work of managing a face that does not match what is happening underneath, what researchers call surface acting, performing one feeling while privately carrying another (Hochschild, 1983). It drains you in ways the job never accounts for. So the leader grows distant. She feels like she is drowning in everyone's expectations and judgments, with nowhere quiet to set it down. And the relationships she carries begin to feel the strain, not because she is incapable or uncaring, but because no one can perform perfection indefinitely without something leaking out sideways.

None of this means good leadership is out of reach. I do not think it comes down to luck at all. It has everything to do with self-awareness and knowing your limitations. A good leader is confident, open to other perspectives, and willing to let people know them in a real way. When you lead like that, people are more inclined to help, and that is what lets you share the load instead of carrying it alone. And these are the very qualities that protect a leader from burnout. The ones who stay open and know their limits tend to hold up over time. The ones who carry it all are often the most exposed.

The leaders who do this well tend to be comfortable in their own skin, at peace with what they know and what they do not, and unbothered by letting others see both. They lean on their own transparency instead of hiding it. And they carry a team mindset, an approach where people grow together and learn together, where the leader sets the tone by example rather than by performance.

This is what researchers call psychological safety, the shared sense that it is safe to speak up, ask questions, and admit you do not have all the answers, and it is one of the strongest predictors of how well a team actually functions (Edmondson, 1999). That is the intersection this chapter keeps pointing back to: you can hold a position of influence and still be a whole person inside it. The two were never supposed to be at odds.

Ministry and the Myth of Tireless Service

If leadership carries a quiet isolation, ministry often carries something else entirely: a language that can make it hard to even recognize what you are feeling as burnout. Pastors, ministry leaders, first ladies, worship leaders, and the women running the ministries nobody puts on the program are often the ones giving the most of themselves, pouring into the work as their own measure of faithfulness. That is exactly why this section matters. Not because service is the problem, but because so many faithful people have quietly confused service with self-sacrifice.

If you serve in ministry, I want to say this plainly, before anything else: this is not a critique of your calling. It is not a suggestion that your service is somehow wrong, or that your leaders have failed you, or that the church has gotten it backward. Most of the time, the yes comes from something beautiful. It comes from love. It comes from a genuine desire to serve the people God has placed in front of you. This section is not about correcting that heart. It is about naming what happens when a hundred faithful yeses, each one good on its own, add up to more than one body was ever meant to carry.

The data on this is sobering. In Barna Group polling of Protestant senior pastors, more than four in ten had seriously considered leaving full-time ministry, and the top reasons named were the immense stress of the role and a pervasive sense of loneliness and isolation (Barna Group, 2022). Duke University's Clergy Health Initiative, which has spent more than a decade studying the well-being of United Methodist clergy in North Carolina, has found higher rates of obesity among pastors than among their fellow North Carolinians, 41% compared with 29%, along with elevated rates of diabetes, arthritis, and other chronic disease, and depression symptoms at nearly double the national average (Duke Clergy Health Initiative, n.d.). Its researchers point to congregational demands and the blurred line between ministry and personal life as significant contributors.

The Flourishing in Ministry project out of the University of Notre Dame reached a similar conclusion from a different angle: pastors with strong boundaries, regular sabbath practice, and support from peers were significantly more likely to be flourishing, not despite those practices, but because of them (M. Bloom, 2019). Rest, in other words, is not the thing that gets in the way of a thriving ministry. It is one of the things that makes one possible.

Loneliness in ministry is not incidental. It is built in. You are surrounded by a congregation, yet always weighing how honest you can really be, because your role is to hold everyone else's crisis, their grief, their marriage, their diagnosis, while rarely feeling free to bring your own. Many people in ministry are also wearing more hats than the title suggests. There is the preaching or teaching, and then there is the counseling, the administration, the visitation, the funerals, the weddings, the budget, the building, the social media, and the expectation of being available at any hour for any need. It is its own form of overfunctioning, wrapped in language about calling and sacrifice that can make it feel almost disrespectful to say, I am tired.

Here is what I want to name gently, because I believe it matters more than almost anything else in this chapter: serving God should never require abandoning the body, mind, and spirit God entrusted to you. Somewhere along the way, many of us absorbed the idea that if we are doing the Lord's work, we are somehow supposed to forgo our own well-being. I had to question whether that belief was actually coming from Scripture, or from what I had learned to associate with faithfulness.

Let me say something plainly, and let me say it as someone who has had to sit with it myself. God never handed anyone a list that said, join a thousand and one ministries, and then I will know you love me. That criterion does not exist. Service is real, and it is part of being in service to the people we love and the gifts we have been given. But the number of ministries you are on was never the measure of your devotion. Many of us have learned to treat it that way.

I know this because I lived it. As a believer, I had to grapple honestly with my own why, the reason underneath all my doing. At one point, I was serving on multiple ministries at the same time, and it became exhausting. I was losing the time and attention that other parts of my life needed from me. What I had to learn, and it did not come easy, was that I was not a lesser Christian for serving on one ministry instead of five. And God didn't love me any less if I only served on one or none. I learned to prioritize my capacity. Because my service to God was never really about how many ministries had my name on the list. It was about being a good steward over what I had been given, caring for my heart, walking in obedience, and treating others well.

This brings us right back to a question from an earlier chapter: the difference between activity and progress, between motion and meaning. The same question belongs here, in the sanctuary. What is the why underneath all the doing? Why do so many of us believe that serving, no matter what it costs our own well-being, is what makes us a good and faithful servant?

The same God who called us to serve also instructed us to rest and to be good stewards over the temple we were given, our own bodies, minds, and spirits. Yes, we are called to go and teach and serve. But nowhere were we told to spread ourselves so thin that there is nothing left.

And if we are honest about it, when we are that depleted, we are not truly of good service to anyone anyway, because we are simply too tired. Running yourself into the ground in the name of ministry is not the same thing as obedience. It may be a story playing in the background of your mind being tied to your identity and your faith. But the blessing is this: the story running in the background can be examined and gently rewritten.

And let me be clear, this is not a call to do less. If you have the capacity to serve in multiple areas of ministry, and it genuinely brings you joy, then by all means, do what you love. Serve fully. This is not about shrinking your service. But if you do not have that capacity, if you are running on empty and calling it faithfulness, I want to gently ask you the same thing I had to ask myself: what do I actually have the capacity to do, and still be in service to God and His people?

Even in the account of creation, God worked for six days and rested on the seventh. Rest was built into the design from the very beginning (Genesis 2:2–3). If rest was part of the design God modeled at creation, it is not a departure from faithfulness. It is an expression of it.

This thread runs throughout Scripture, not just at creation. After the prophet Elijah's greatest spiritual victory, a confrontation with hundreds of false prophets on Mount Carmel, he collapsed into exhaustion and despair, telling God he wanted to die. God's response was not a rebuke and it was not a bigger assignment. God sent an angel to let him sleep, then wake him to eat and drink, then let him sleep again, before he had the strength to travel forty days and forty nights to Horeb (1 Kings 19:4-8). Before God spoke to Elijah, God fed him and let him rest.

Restoration came before revelation.

Jesus modeled this same rhythm. Even in the middle of a ministry with constant demand and constant need, he regularly withdrew to quiet places to pray (Luke 5:16), and he instructed his own disciples, when they were worn down from ministry, to come away by themselves and rest a while (Mark 6:31). It is the same invitation he extends more broadly: Come to me, all who are weary and burdened, and I will give you rest (Matthew 11:28). That invitation was never reserved for people outside the church. It was, and is, for the ones carrying it.

The psalmist writes that God gives sleep to those He loves (Psalm 127:2), and there is a quiet wisdom in Ecclesiastes that better is one handful with peace than two handfuls with toil and a chasing after the wind (Ecclesiastes 4:6). And there is Psalm 23, so familiar it can lose its weight: the Lord as shepherd who leads us beside still waters and restores our soul, who prepares provision even in the presence of pressure, until, as the psalm puts it, our cup runs over (Psalm 23:2-5). That overflow is not possible from a cup that is empty. You cannot pour from what you have not first allowed to be filled.

Sometimes we confuse carrying our cross with carrying everything.

Faithfulness is not measured by exhaustion. Rest is not a reward you earn after enough sacrifice. Rest is part of faithful stewardship.

Serving from an empty vessel is not sustainable, and it was never the model. A shepherd who never rests cannot see clearly, cannot lead well, and eventually cannot show up at all. Ministry burnout does not just cost the leader. It costs the very people that leader was called to serve, because depletion has a ceiling on what it can give.

This is starting to shift, and it deserves to be named with hope. A growing number of churches in the Black community, across denominations, are hosting wellness conferences and building mental health ministries, not only for congregants navigating stress and mental health challenges, but for the lay workers, the pastors, the ministers, and the deacons carrying the weight behind the scenes.

Balm in Gilead, founded in 1989 by Dr. Pernessa C. Seele, has spent decades convening its annual Healthy Churches conference, bringing together clergy and members of African American faith organizations across multiple denominations to address health disparities, mental health included, in partnership with public health agencies. Baptist churches have been part of this movement directly. Two African American Baptist congregations in New Jersey piloted the Promoting Emotional Wellness and Spirituality program, a training curriculum that helps churches build a Mental Health Ministry Committee and reduce stigma around treatment for depression (Williams et al., 2014). In the Bay Area, Kaiser Permanente's Project Trust trained leaders across dozens of Black churches, Baptist congregations among them, in mental health first aid, and helped pastors integrate mental health directly into sermons rather than treating it as a subject outside the church's scope.

Suicide prevention specifically has become a growing focus. Soul Shop for Black Churches, a curriculum developed and delivered by Black faith leaders trained in suicide prevention, was added to the Suicide Prevention Resource Center's Best Practices Registry (Suicide Prevention Resource Center, 2025). That urgency is grounded in real numbers. CDC youth survey data show that suicide attempts have been higher among Black high school students than among their peers from most other groups, and that in 2021, Black female students had a higher prevalence of suicide attempts than White female students (Gaylor et al., 2023). If you or someone you love is carrying thoughts of suicide, please hear this: you do not have to carry them alone, and support is available right now through the 988 Suicide and Crisis Lifeline, by call or text, any hour of any day.

Within the Apostolic and Pentecostal tradition, the Church of God in Christ, the largest predominantly African American Pentecostal denomination in the country, launched its first national mental health public service campaign in 2024 in partnership with the U.S. Department of Health and Human Services' Partnership Center, directly naming the stigma many in ministry carry (Church of God in Christ, 2024).

This same reckoning is happening in the Muslim community, including in Black Muslim spaces within our urban communities. Research on imams in the United States has found that the overwhelming majority spend significant time each week providing informal counseling to congregants navigating depression, grief, and family crisis, functioning as first responders to mental health needs with little support for their own wellness in the process (Ali et al., 2005). In response, mosques in cities like Detroit have begun opening on-site mental health clinics staffed by Muslim clinicians. And since 2015, the Muslim Wellness Foundation has hosted its annual Black Muslim Psychology Conference, the only gathering of its kind, to address the specific mental health needs and stigma within Black Muslim communities.

What all of this points to is the same truth this chapter keeps returning to: those who serve, in any tradition, in any pulpit, on any ministry team, are not exempt from needing care themselves. The fact that this is now being said out loud, in conference rooms and from pulpits, in Baptist, Apostolic, and Muslim spaces alike, is not a departure from faith. It is faith communities making room for what people in ministry and the communities they serve have needed all along.

If you serve in ministry and you recognize yourself in this chapter, you are not lacking in faith. You are human, doing sacred work inside a body and a nervous system that were never designed to run without rest. Naming that is not a crisis of belief. It may be the beginning of a more sustainable one, and a more honest yes the next time someone asks.

Interrupting the Pattern

You may not be able to change every system you are in overnight. But you can begin to change your relationship with those systems. You can begin to notice when you are operating from pressure instead of purpose. You can question the belief that you have to do something first to rest. You can recognize when you are overfunctioning instead of simply functioning, and when a room is asking for more of you than it has any right to ask.

Change does not require perfection or a complete life overhaul. It begins with small, intentional shifts. Research in positive psychology suggests that even brief positive emotional experiences can regulate stress and build resilience over time (Fredrickson, 2001). That means moments of rest, joy, and genuine pause are not insignificant. They are foundational. Sometimes healing does not look like a breakthrough. Sometimes it looks like a breath.

By now, you have moved through the psychology of pushing through, the wounds that feed it, the cultural messages that reinforce it, the systems and professions that sustain it, and the roles that isolate us most. Somewhere in one of these rooms you may have recognized yourself. Not as someone who failed to carry enough. As someone who was never shown where her capacity ended, and everyone else's expectations began.

Perhaps the question was never whether you were strong enough to carry it all. Perhaps the better question is whether you were ever meant to.

Before we go further, before this book moves into the territory of burnout within your relationships, your caregiving roles, and your inner world, take a moment. Not to fix what you have read. Not to immediately create a plan. Just to notice what came up. What felt familiar. What you have been carrying that now has a name, the way Yvonne's did.

That awareness is not small. That is the beginning of change.

Chapter Summary

Yvonne was not weak, and she was not failing. She was standing in two roles built to receive everyone else's weight while offering nowhere to set down her own.

1. **Leadership can be lonely by design.** The higher you rise, the harder it can be to know who you can truly be honest with. In middle management, that can feel especially complicated. You may be unsure who you can trust above you because you do not want to appear incapable or as though you cannot handle your role. At the same time, you may hold back with the people you lead because you do not want to lose their confidence or respect.

2. **Isolation is not a personal failing.** It is built into roles that ask you to hold everyone while being held by no one. Naming it is not weakness. It is accuracy.

3. **The mask is expensive.** When you do not feel safe being fully yourself, you perform certainty, competence, and having it all together, and that performance burns through the capacity you have left.

4. **Service is a blessing, not a mandate to disappear.** Serving others is sacred and real. But no faith required you to wear yourself thin in its name. Joining every ministry was never the measure of your devotion.

5. **You were never meant to be the only one who carries and is never carried.** The rooms learned to lean on you because you became the dependable one. You are allowed to need what you so freely give.

Hard Truth

Everyone knows they can lean on you. But when was the last time you had someone you could lean on? **Share your thoughts below.**

CAPACITY CHECK

Who Holds You?

Take a moment to sit with what came up as you read this chapter, especially if you are someone others describe as strong, dependable, or unshakeable. Notice what you feel in your body when you consider setting some of it down.

1. When I am overwhelmed in my role, who do I actually have to be honest with? If the answer is no one, what has that cost me?

2. Where am I performing certainty or competence that I do not feel within, and what would it take to let even one person see the truth?

3. Have I taken on roles or ministries that are quietly costing me more than I have to give? Did God, or my own sense of obligation, actually ask that of me?

4. Do I believe rest is a departure from faithfulness, or a part of it? Where did that belief come from?

5. Where in my life am I demanding a level of perfection no one is actually required to carry, and what would it look like to offer myself the same grace I extend to everyone else?

Chapter 7

Burnout Beyond the Office

When Love, Caregiving, and Relationships Become the Source of Depletion

"Love is a combination of care,
commitment, knowledge, responsibility, respect and trust."
~ bell hooks

Veronica did not realize how exhausted she was until she stood in the middle of a grocery store aisle and cried because she could not remember what she came to buy. She had not had a bad day. She had had a thousand ordinary ones. Ones where she got her mother dressed, prepared medications, navigated a doctor's appointment, answered calls from her teenage daughter's school, answered texts from her husband who needed something, answered emails from her supervisor who also needed something, and then, somehow, kept going. She did not call what she felt burnout. She called it life.

But something in her, something quiet and persistent, already knew. The conversation about burnout most often centers on work. On the career that demands too much, the workplace that does not give enough, the professional role that eventually consumes the person filling it.

That conversation is real, necessary, and long overdue. But it is incomplete.

Because burnout does not check your badge before it settles into your body. It does not ask whether your exhaustion came from a client meeting or from two hours of sitting with a parent whose memory keeps slipping away. It does not distinguish between the depletion that follows a hard quarter at work and the depletion that follows years of loving someone whose needs consistently exceed your capacity to meet them. The physiological experience may look similar.

The cost to your nervous system can be significant in both. The impact on your identity, your sense of self, and your ability to continue can be profound regardless of where depletion began.

What differs is that when burnout comes from caregiving, from relationships, from parenting, or from the accumulated weight of showing up for others in your most personal spaces, it carries an additional layer of silence. Because in those spaces, you are not supposed to be depleted. You are supposed to be devoted. This chapter exists to name what many people have been living without language for.

Burnout Is Not Only Occupational

As previously mentioned, the World Health Organization classifies burnout as an occupational phenomenon, a syndrome resulting from chronic workplace stress that has not been successfully managed (World Health Organization, 2019). This classification has been enormously valuable in legitimizing the experience for millions of people who have struggled to name their exhaustion in professional contexts. However, the clinical and popular conversation has increasingly recognized that chronic depletion does not confine itself to professional domains.

What researchers are increasingly finding is that burnout is really a response to chronic, unmanaged demands in any part of life that asks for sustained emotional, cognitive, and physical investment (Maslach & Leiter, 2016; Mikolajczak & Roskam, 2018). When those demands consistently exceed available resources, whether in a boardroom or a caregiving home, the result follows the same neurobiological pattern. The same stress systems activate, the same cumulative wear accrues, and the same sense of depletion, detachment, and diminished efficacy emerges (McEwen, 2007).

Burnout, understood more broadly, is the body's response to prolonged giving without adequate restoration. It is what happens when the demands on you exceed your capacity for long enough that the exceeding becomes ordinary. And in many lives, the most relentless demands do not come from the workplace.

They come from the people you love.

Caregiver: The Invisible Labor of Love

There is a particular kind of exhaustion that comes from caring for someone who cannot fully care for themselves. It may be an aging parent whose cognitive decline requires your constant navigation. It may be a child with complex medical or developmental needs whose care is ongoing and without a clear horizon. It may be a spouse or partner navigating chronic illness or mental health challenges who needs from you what you are not always resourced to give.

Whatever the specific relationship, caregiver burnout is one of the most underrecognized and underaddressed forms of depletion in contemporary life. Research consistently confirms the severity of this experience. A meta-analysis found that informal caregivers, those providing unpaid care for family members or loved ones, experience significantly elevated rates of depression, anxiety, and physical health deterioration compared to non-caregiving adults (Pinquart & Sörensen, 2003).

Caregivers of individuals with dementia, in particular, demonstrate measurable changes in cortisol patterns and immune functioning consistent with chronic stress exposure (Roepke et al., 2011). The body of a caregiver is not simply tired. It is physiologically altered by the sustained demands of the role.

What makes caregiver burnout particularly difficult to name is the emotional complexity it carries. Unlike professional burnout, where frustration with a job or an organization feels relatively acceptable, caregiver burnout is accompanied by guilt, shame, and the belief that feeling depleted is a betrayal of love. You are exhausted by the person you love most. That feels unspeakable. So you do not speak it. You continue. And the cost compounds.

Researchers describe this as role captivity, the experience of feeling trapped in a role one did not fully anticipate and cannot exit without significant consequence (Pearlin et al., 1990). Richard Schulz's decades of research on caregiver stress, including the landmark Caregiver Health Effects Study, have been foundational in documenting the toll of this dynamic (Schulz & Beach, 1999). This sense of being bound to the role without adequate support or relief is one of the strongest predictors of caregiver burnout and has been associated with increased rates of depression, physical illness, and, in extreme cases, premature mortality in caregivers.

Veronica was not a bad daughter. She had not failed at anything. She was a woman whose love had been given without boundary, without support, and without the understanding that love does not protect the body from the physiological consequences of sustained depletion. Nobody had ever asked her what she had the capacity to carry, and the roles kept arriving anyway. Loving someone does not make you immune to burnout. In some cases, it makes you more vulnerable to it.

A Note for Caregivers

If you are caring for someone, a parent, a child, a partner, or a sibling, this chapter was written with you in mind.

The particular exhaustion of caregiver burnout is that it arrives wrapped in love, which makes it almost impossible to name without guilt. You are not less devoted for being depleted. You are not failing the person you love by seeking respite for yourself. You are a human being doing something hard out of love, often with no one seeing it. The most sustainable care you can offer is care that does not require you to erase yourself. Your needs are not competing with your love. They are what make it last.

Parental Burnout: When Raising Children Empties You

Parenting is one of the most profound and meaningful roles a human being can inhabit. It is also, in contemporary culture, one of the most exhausting. Parental burnout is a relatively recently named phenomenon, though the experience itself is ancient. It is defined by researchers Isabelle Roskam and Moïra Mikolajczak (2020) as a specific burnout syndrome resulting from the chronic imbalance between the demands of the parenting role and the resources available to meet them. Like occupational burnout, parental burnout manifests across three dimensions: emotional exhaustion in the parenting role; emotional distancing from one's children, a felt reduction in the warmth and presence one can offer; and a diminished sense of parenting efficacy, the nagging sense that one is not doing enough or being enough.

Their research, conducted across forty-two countries and involving over seventeen thousand parents, found that parental burnout is not a rare or marginal experience. It affects parents across cultures, socioeconomic levels, and family configurations (Roskam et al., 2021), and researchers have found its consequences extend beyond the parent's well-being to include meaningful effects on children's emotional security and behavioral outcomes (Mikolajczak et al., 2018).

High-achieving parents face a particular version of this pressure. Many have internalized extraordinarily high standards not only for their professional performance but for their parenting as well. They want to be present, engaged, supportive, fun, emotionally attuned, academically reinforcing, spiritually grounding, nutritionally responsible, and available, all while managing careers, households, and the infrastructure of daily life. The standard is impossible. And the gap between that standard and reality becomes its own source of chronic stress.

Research on what has been called intensive parenting ideology, the cultural expectation that parents, and mothers in particular, should invest maximal time, energy, and resources into their children's development, shows that adherence to this ideology is associated with poorer maternal mental health, including greater stress and depression and lower life satisfaction (Rizzo et al., 2013). The very commitment to parenting well, when it becomes an unrelenting standard without grace, becomes the source of the exhaustion.

For single parents, parents of children with complex needs, and parents navigating their own unresolved trauma, the demands are compounded. When you are trying to give your children what you did not receive, while simultaneously managing the grief of not having received it, the emotional labor is immense. And in most cases, it is invisible. You are expected to do it quietly, consistently, and with gratitude.

And here is something the culture does not give us much room to say. You can love your children with everything in you and still be exhausted by the role. You can adore the person you are caring for and still feel worn down by the caregiving. Both things are true at once. But the moment you admit it, the moment you say you are tired, or that some days you did not want to do it, someone is right there to remind you that this is your job. You are supposed to do these things. As if being supposed to do something means it does not cost you anything. It does. And over years of giving everyone else what they need, a lot of people look up one day and realize they do not know who they are anymore. They lost their dreams somewhere in the caretaking. They lost the things they used to want. They gave so much of themselves to everyone else that there was no self left over.

If that is you, you are not selfish for noticing it. You are honest. And what you do with these feelings matters, which is exactly why the next chapter is about boundaries, because boundaries, the kind grounded in your own values and what actually feels right to you, are how you stop disappearing inside the roles you love.

Relational Burnout: When Love Becomes Labor

Relationships, even healthy and loving ones, require emotional energy. The investment of attention, vulnerability, empathy, patience, and repair that sustaining connection requires is real work, even when that work is chosen and reciprocated. When the balance of giving and receiving in a relationship shifts significantly, or when one person carries disproportionate responsibility for the emotional health and functioning of a partnership, relational burnout can develop.

Relational burnout shares characteristics with its occupational counterpart: emotional exhaustion, growing detachment, and a diminished sense of efficacy in the relationship. Research on emotional labor, the concept sociologist Arlie Hochschild introduced in Chapter 4's discussion of the mental load, the management of one's own feelings in service of another's emotional needs or relational expectations, has documented the significant toll this invisible work takes on those who bear it most heavily (Hochschild, 1983). In the decades since Hochschild's foundational work, researchers have consistently found that women carry a disproportionate share of emotional and domestic labor within intimate relationships and family systems, and that marriage itself continues to deliver a better deal to men than to women (Dempsey, 2002).

This is not only about romantic partnerships. Relational burnout can emerge in friendships where one person is consistently the listener, the advisor, the caretaker of another's emotional world. It can emerge in families where one sibling bears the weight of maintaining connection and managing dynamics that everyone else avoids. It can emerge in any relationship where your presence, your empathy, and your emotional attunement are consistently required without adequate reciprocity.

For many high-achieving women, relational exhaustion is further amplified by what researchers have called the second shift, the continuation of domestic and relational labor after the paid workday ends (Hochschild & Machung, 2012). Even in dual-income households, studies consistently show that women continue to carry significantly more of the household management, emotional coordination, and invisible mental load. The result is a life that is never fully off duty, a body and mind that are never fully at rest, and an identity that has been so thoroughly organized around being available to others that it struggles to remember what it needs for itself.

I lived inside that pattern for a long time. I was trying to be all things to everybody, the one who showed up, the one who fixed it, the one who was always available no matter what it cost me. And I want to be honest about something, because we do not say it often enough: your relationships can burn you out too. Not because the people are bad, and not because love is the problem. But because being everything for everyone, all the time, is not sustainable, no matter how much you care about them.

I had to learn that being constantly available was not the same as being loving. It was just a habit I had confused with love. When I finally stopped auto-piloting into everyone else's needs and started asking whether I actually had the capacity to give what was being asked, my relationships did not fall apart. The real ones got healthier. And the ones that only worked when I was overextending myself, well, those told me something too.

Here is the part we do not always want to say out loud. Relationships come with sacrifice; that is true, but they are also supposed to have reciprocity. When you are the only one giving, and it is not coming back, the relationship starts to feel lopsided, and that imbalance is its own kind of stress. It wears on you. And if we are being honest, sometimes there is something underneath the constant giving. Sometimes we overcompensate, and then quietly grow bitter and resentful when no one pours back into us. That is worth sitting with.

Why am I always the one giving and doing? What am I actually seeking by it? That is a bigger question than this book can answer, and honestly it might be a book of its own. But I raise it here because overextending yourself in your relationships, without ever asking why, is a straight path to burnout. You just may not recognize it as burnout, because it is wearing the face of love.

The Shared Reserve

It helps to picture it. Imagine one reserve at the center of your life, and every role you hold reaching into it. The job. The person you care for. The children. The relationship. Not four separate accounts, four withdrawals from the same one. That is why a hard week at work leaves you with less patience at home, and why a season of caregiving makes the job feel heavier than it was. Nothing has been added. Something has been spent, and it was all coming from the same place.

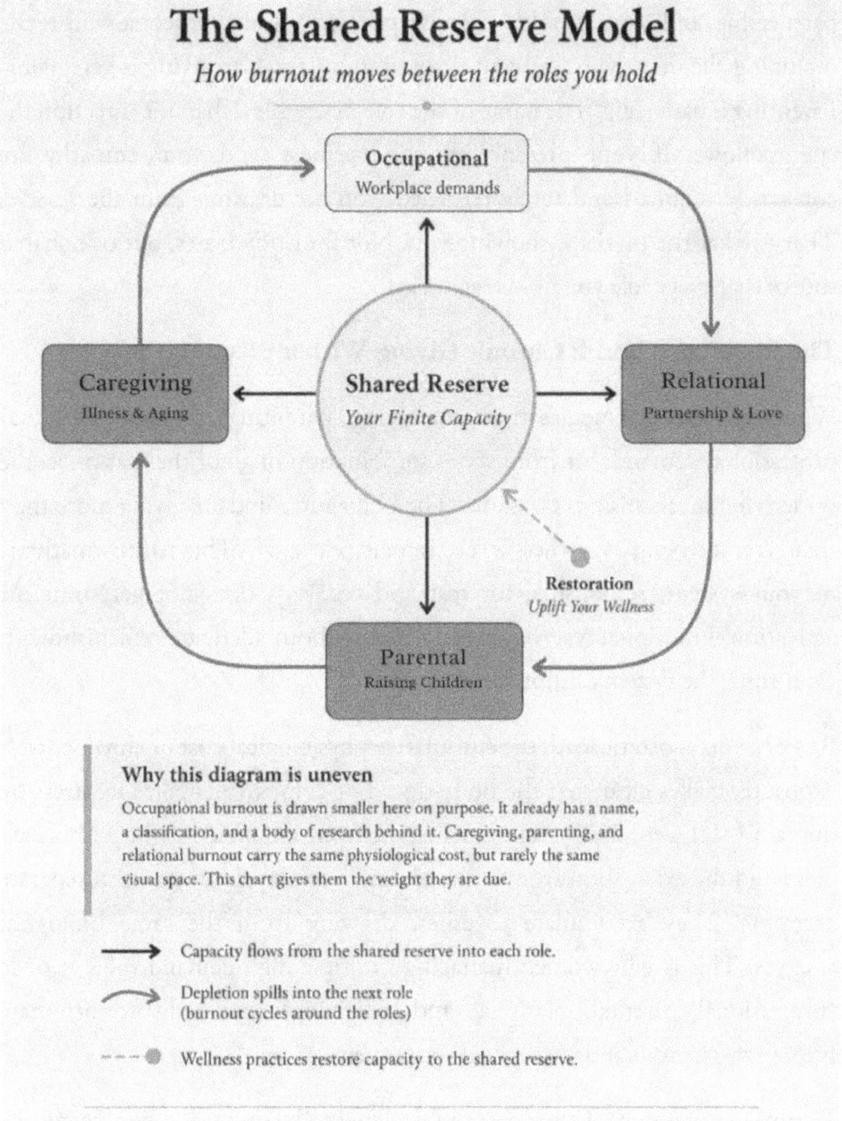

Figure 7.1. Shared Reserve Model

You may look at the reserve and not see your particular role named on it. If the weight you carry comes from ministry, from leading a team, from being the one your community turns to, it still belongs here. The four labels are broader than they look. Occupational is not only workplace demands; it holds leadership and the pressure of being the one others answer to. Relational is not only partnership and love; it holds friendship, family, and the people you serve, including the ones who find you through ministry. Caregiving is caregiving. Parenting is parenting. The name of the role matters less than the direction the energy flows. If your presence, your steadiness, and your empathy are constantly required and rarely returned, you are drawing from the reserve. That is what the model is showing you. Not four tidy boxes, but one shared source that every role you hold reaches into.

The Common Thread: Chronic Giving Without Restoration

Whether burnout emerges from caregiving, parenting, relational labor, or professional demands, or from some combination of all of them at once, the underlying mechanism is the same. The body and mind are giving more than they are receiving. Cortisol levels remain elevated. The parasympathetic nervous system, responsible for rest and recovery, does not get sufficient activation. Emotional reserves are depleted without adequate replenishment. Over time, the system cannot sustain itself.

Research on allostatic load, the cumulative physiological cost of chronic stress exposure, makes clear that the body does not compartmentalize its stress by domain (McEwen, 2007). The exhaustion from a difficult night with a sick child and the exhaustion from a demanding workday do not exist in separate accounts. They accumulate together, drawing from the same biological reserves. This is why women managing multiple high-demand roles at once (professional, parental, relational, and caregiving) carry a disproportionate burden of burnout and its physical consequences.

Compassion fatigue, distinct from but related to burnout, is a significant risk for those whose life roles require sustained empathic attunement. Psychologist Kristin Neff's research, widely applied in burnout recovery, points to self-compassion practices as a primary buffer against this kind of depletion (Neff, 2011). When your daily existence requires you to be present to others' pain, need, or vulnerability, whether professionally or personally, the emotional cost is real and must be actively managed. Without deliberate practices of self-replenishment, the capacity for empathy diminishes. Not because you have stopped caring, but because the system that allows you to feel and respond to others' needs has been stretched beyond its sustainable range.

The version of you that is available to love others well, that can parent with presence, care for a loved one with patience, and sustain deep relationships with genuine warmth, requires that version of you to be resourced. That is not a luxury. That is a physiological prerequisite.

Why This Goes Unnamed

There are several reasons why burnout in these domains remains unspoken for so many people, and it is worth naming them directly. The first is cultural expectation. Many women have been raised in environments, and in a broader culture, that frames self-sacrifice in relational roles as a virtue. Mothers who are exhausted are expected to be grateful. Caregivers who are depleted are expected to be selfless. Partners who are emotionally empty are expected to remain giving. The cultural narrative around these roles does not create space for burnout, because burnout implies that the demands are too great, and that acknowledgment challenges the myth that love is inexhaustible.

The second is the absence of a legitimizing framework. Occupational burnout has the validation of organizational research, clinical recognition, and, increasingly, institutional acknowledgment. Parental burnout is beginning to receive similar attention. But relational and caregiving burnout remain relatively invisible in popular discourse. Without language and cultural validation, many people who are experiencing these forms of depletion conclude that something must be wrong with them, that they are not strong enough, not loving enough, not capable enough, when in reality, they are simply human beings whose systems have been exceeded.

The third is guilt. Naming burnout in intimate contexts feels, to many, like a complaint against the people they love. It can trigger grief about the quality of love and presence they are able to offer. It can feel like a failure of devotion.

This guilt keeps the experience buried, and buried experience does not heal. It compounds.

There is a fourth reason, and it is quieter than the other three. Somewhere along the way you learned to do it yourself.

If I do not do it myself, it will not get done, or it will not get done right. Most of us have said some version of that sentence, and most of us have said it with pride. It sounds like competence. It sounds like knowing your own standards. What it usually is, underneath, is something older: a lesson learned in a season when needing someone was not safe, or when the person you needed did not come.

Hyper-independence is not a personality trait. It is a trauma adaptation.

That distinction matters here more than almost anywhere else in this book, because caregiving and parenting and partnership are exactly the places where help is available and refused. The refusal does not feel like refusing. It feels like handling it. But doing it all yourself does not expand your capacity. It only hides how far past it you already are, and it hides it from the people most willing to help.

What you have been feeling is not a character deficiency. It is a physiological reality that has been dismissed because it did not come with a performance review.

Applying the S.O.U.L. Framework to Non-Occupational Burnout

The S.O.U.L. Framework™, which Chapter 10 explores in depth, is not designed exclusively for professional depletion. Its four phases apply with equal relevance to burnout that emerges from caregiving, parenting, and relational labor, and in some ways, those contexts make the framework's invitation even more essential.

Speak Your Truth, in these contexts, means allowing yourself to say out loud what has likely been unspeakable. I am exhausted by caring for my mother. I love my children and I am burned out by parenting them. I am depleted by this relationship. These sentences feel dangerous because they risk being heard as the withdrawal of love. But speaking the truth of your experience is not a withdrawal of love. It is a prerequisite for continuing to love sustainably. You cannot give from what you do not have. Acknowledging your depletion is the first step toward replenishing it.

Own Your Story, here, means examining the patterns and beliefs that have allowed your needs to become invisible in these relationships. Where did you learn that your needs were secondary to everyone else's? Whose model of caregiving, mothering, or partnering are you unconsciously performing? What fear lives beneath the inability to ask for help or to set a limit on what you give? Understanding these patterns does not require you to stop loving. It requires you to understand why love, for you, has come to mean erasure of self.

Uplift Your Wellness, in relational and caregiving contexts, requires building practices of replenishment that are not conditional on others' stability or approval. This may mean accessing respite care. It may mean establishing time that belongs entirely to you within a partnership. It may mean returning to practices of spiritual, creative, or physical care that have been abandoned in service of others' needs. It means treating your restoration as a non-negotiable rather than something you will attend to eventually.

Live in Your Truth, applied to these relationships, does not mean freedom from love or responsibility. It means freedom from the belief that your worth in these relationships is contingent on how much of yourself you can give away. It means relationships characterized by genuine reciprocity, honest communication about capacity and need, and the understanding that your well-being is not opposed to your love. It is what makes your love sustainable.

You Are Allowed to Need Something Back

One of the most transformative recognitions for individuals navigating non-occupational burnout is permission. Specifically, the permission to have needs within relationships and roles that have been constructed around giving.

Research on caregiver support systems consistently demonstrates that caregivers with stronger social support and a greater sense of confidence in their caregiving role, what researchers call caregiving self-efficacy, report significantly lower burden, and the people they care for report a meaningfully better quality of life, than caregivers without that support (Leung et al., 2020).

Effective caregiving, effective parenting, and effective partnership all require someone resourced enough to remain present, responsive, and regulated. The sacrifice of your own well-being does not, over time, improve the quality of care you offer. It diminishes it. This means that asking for help is not a weakness or a failure of the role. It is a strategy for sustaining it.

Building in respite, naming your limits, accepting support, redistributing labor within partnerships, and seeking professional support for caregiving and parenting challenges are not signs that you love less.

They are the practices that make it possible to keep loving.

You are allowed to be a devoted mother who also needs time away from her children. You are allowed to love your aging parent deeply and still need someone else to take a turn. You are allowed to be fully committed to a relationship and still require emotional reciprocity within it.

These are not contradictions. They are the conditions under which genuine, sustained love becomes possible.

Burnout, wherever it arises, tells the same truth: something has been given without being restored for too long. The source of the giving does not change that truth. What changes is what you decide to do with it.

Veronica is doing this too. Slowly. Imperfectly. She still cries sometimes, though less often in parking lots. She has not stopped loving her mother, and she has not stopped being tired. Both are true. She is learning that both can be true without one canceling out the other. That may be the most honest definition of healing this chapter can offer.

Chapter Summary

Veronica's exhaustion was never a failure of love. It was the cost of loving without boundary, without support, and without anyone ever asking what she had the capacity to carry.

1. **Burnout does not stay at work.** The clinical definition centers the workplace, but chronic demands outside of work can create significant depletion too.

2. **Caregiver burnout arrives wrapped in love.** That is what makes it nearly impossible to name. Being exhausted by the person you love most feels unspeakable, so it goes unspoken, and the cost compounds in silence.
3. **Parental burnout is real and it is measurable.** It has its own three dimensions, its own research base, and its own impossible standard: the expectation to be present, engaged, and endlessly available while running everything else.
4. **Love becomes labor when the giving stops going both ways.** Relational burnout builds wherever your empathy and attunement are required without reciprocity, in partnerships, friendships, and families alike.
5. **It all draws from one reserve.** The roles are separate. The capacity they spend is not. That is why depletion in one place shows up as impatience, distance, or exhaustion somewhere else entirely.
6. **Doing it all yourself is not the solution.** Hyper-independence looks like strength and functions like a wall. It does not increase what you have. It only hides how little is left.
7. **You are allowed to need something back.** Asking for help is not a failure of devotion. It is the condition under which devotion remains possible.

You do not have to choose between love and well-being. You have to choose the version of yourself that can sustain both.

Hard Truth

> Burnout does not check your badge before it settles into your body. The question is: Where is your depletion really coming from?

CAPACITY CHECK

Write Without Judgment

Before continuing, pause and sit with what arose as you read this chapter. Many people reach this section and recognize for the first time that their exhaustion has had a name all along. Others recognize that what they have been managing is not one source of depletion but several, layered and interlocking in ways they had not previously examined.

This is not a moment for self-criticism or for analyzing what you should have done differently. It is a moment for honest recognition.

Where is your burnout really coming from?

Journaling Prompts

1. The role that has depleted me most, outside of work, is...
2. I have never allowed myself to say that I am burned out by... because...
3. What I need in order to continue showing up in this role is...
4. The permission I have been waiting for in this relationship or role is...

Chapter 8

Why Your Body Starts Yelling

What Burnout Does to Your Mind, Body, and Spirit

"Your mind can lie. Your body will not."
~ Dr. Tashina Reeder

Monica, from Chapter 5, laughed when she said it, but her hand stayed pressed against her temple. She had just wrapped her third meeting of the morning, skipped breakfast, and was halfway through a lukewarm coffee she kept forgetting to drink. Her calendar was full, her inbox was fuller, and her patience was gone. When someone casually said, "It's probably just stress," she nodded, smiled, and kept going. But later that night, lying in bed wide awake, staring at the ceiling while her body refused to rest, she realized something. This was not just stress. This was her body trying to get her attention. And if she was honest, it had been trying to get her attention for a long time.

Twenty minutes earlier, in that third meeting, Monica had snapped at her marketing coordinator over a font size. A font size. She heard the sharpness in her own voice before she could stop it. She saw the coordinator's face shift, that small flinch people do when they are recalibrating how safe it is to talk to you.

Monica knew, even as it was happening, that this was not really about the font. But she could not find her way back to gentle in time to fix it before the call ended. She told herself it was a small thing. It was not the first small thing that week.

Moments like this do not happen in isolation. They are often the continuation of patterns we have already explored. The conditioning to push, the identity tied to being strong, the pressure to perform, and the deeper layers of what has been carried over time all build beneath the surface. By the time the body begins to interrupt you, it is rarely the beginning of the story. It is the moment your body can no longer carry what your mind has been trying to manage.

Let's start with a truth most women learn the hard way. Your mind can lie. Your body will not. Your mind will say you are fine. Your calendar will confirm you are busy. Your body, however, will tell the truth about what you have left.

The longer you ignore your body, the louder it has to yell to be heard.

Here is why that matters more than it sounds. Every other chapter in this book has asked you to notice your capacity. This is the chapter about the instrument you use to read it.

Your body is the only instrument you have for measuring capacity. When you stop trusting it, you lose the only honest reading you had.

You cannot think your way to an accurate answer about how much you have left. Your mind will consult your calendar, your obligations, and your sense of what a capable woman should be able to handle, and it will return the answer you need to hear rather than the one that is true. Your body does not do that. It has no interest in what you are supposed to be able to carry. It only reports what carrying it is actually costing.

In the previous chapters, we explored why you keep pushing, including conditioning, identity, the productivity trap, and the wound beneath the drive.

This chapter is where all of that lands. Your body has been carrying more than your schedule and responsibilities. It has been carrying your patterns, your pressure, your unprocessed emotions, and your survival strategies. Eventually, the body responds. It does not respond to betray you, but because it refuses to let you disappear inside your own life.

Your Nervous System: Survival Was Never Meant to Be Permanent

Your nervous system is one of the first places burnout begins to show itself. At its core, it operates between activation and restoration. Activation, often referred to as the fight-or-flight response, is your body's go mode. It allows you to problem-solve, multitask, produce, and push through challenges. It is necessary and adaptive. However, it was never designed to be your permanent state.

The opposing state, often called rest-and-digest, is where the body restores. Breathing slows, muscles relax, digestion improves, and healing processes begin. The issue is not that you enter activation; the issue is that you have remained there for extended periods of time. When the stress response stays chronically activated, cortisol tends to remain elevated, signaling to the body that there is always something to manage or survive (McEwen, 2007). Over time, this can make it difficult for the body to recognize or return to calm. This is why, when you finally sit down, you do not always feel relaxed. You feel restless.

Stillness can feel unfamiliar, and at times even uncomfortable, because your body has adapted to functioning in a constant state of urgency.

There is a name for what happens next, and you will meet it again in Chapter 11. Rest anxiety is what it feels like when your body finally gets the stillness it has been asking for and cannot settle into it. You sit down and your chest tightens. You take the afternoon off and spend it mentally reviewing everything you are not doing. The rest is available. Your nervous system simply has not been given permission to receive it yet.

If that sounds familiar, it is not evidence that you are bad at resting. It is evidence of how long you have gone without it.

The Physiology of Stress: What Burnout Does to the Body

Burnout is not just emotional; it is physiological. When stress becomes chronic, it begins to affect multiple systems in the body. Prolonged exposure to elevated cortisol has been associated with increased risk of cardiovascular disease, weakened immune functioning, metabolic disorders, and cognitive decline (McEwen, 2007). This cumulative impact is referred to as allostatic load, which represents the wear and tear on the body associated with repeated exposure to stress.

Research continues to reinforce the seriousness of chronic stress. The American Psychological Association's Stress in America 2023 report described chronic stress as associated with hypertension, heart disease, and stroke, as well as with increased risk for anxiety, depression, and sleep disturbances (American Psychological Association, 2023). Over time, the body remains in a heightened state of alert, which can reduce its ability to recover effectively. Stress does not simply influence how you feel; it is associated with changes in how your body functions. When recovery is consistently delayed, the body begins to compensate in unsustainable ways.

Unprocessed Emotions Live in the Body

The body responds not only to what you do, but also to what you do not process. When you say you are fine while feeling overwhelmed, your body registers that. When you minimize your emotions or push past your limits, your body can reflect the impact. Unprocessed emotions do not simply disappear. The effort in suppressing them can show up physiologically.

Research in psychophysiology has found that emotional suppression is associated with increased physiological stress responses, including elevated heart rate, muscle tension, and prolonged nervous system activation (Gross & Levenson, 1997). This suggests that when emotions are not processed cognitively, they are often carried physically.

This is why stress often shows up in the shoulders, jaw, chest, and stomach. Over time, the mental and physical strain of repeatedly suppressing or pushing through emotions can become difficult to ignore.

How You Learned to Stop Listening

Most of us did not lose touch with our bodies all at once. We were taught, gradually and with good intentions, that the body's signals were an inconvenience to manage rather than information to use.

You learned it when you were told to push through. When finishing mattered more than how you felt while finishing. When the tired was inconvenient, so you overrode it, and nothing bad happened, so you overrode it again. Each override worked, which is exactly why the habit stuck. Your body kept sending the signal and you kept proving you could function without it.

Eventually the signal gets quieter, or you get better at not hearing it. Either way, the reading stops being available to you. That is the real cost of disconnection. Not that you feel less, but that you can no longer tell how much you have left until you have already run out.

I worked with a healthcare administrator who managed a department, a household, and an aging parent, and who described herself as fine every time anyone asked. She had a headache most days. She had stopped noticing it the way you stop noticing traffic noise. She was not ignoring her body out of carelessness. She had simply been running on empty for so long that empty had become her baseline, and she had no reference point left for what full used to feel like.

She ended up hospitalized. Not from one dramatic event, but from the accumulation of everything she had been overriding. What she said afterward has stayed with me: she had not known she was near her limit, because she had not checked in years.

You cannot budget a resource you have stopped measuring.

Burnout Doesn't Just Wear You Out. It Wears Down Your Filter.

Ask any exhausted woman what she said in a group text at 11 p.m. and whether she'd stand by it on a good day, and you will learn most of what you need to know about what burnout does to emotional intelligence.

Emotional intelligence is not a personality trait you either have or don't. It is a set of functions: reading your own emotional state, managing that state, reading the emotional states of others, and navigating relationships with some measure of grace under pressure. Those functions live largely in the prefrontal cortex, the part of the brain responsible for regulation, judgment, and perspective-taking. And the prefrontal cortex happens to be among the first parts of the brain to lose ground under chronic stress. Research shows that stress hormones can weaken prefrontal cortex function while strengthening the more reactive, instinct-driven circuitry of the amygdala (Arnsten, 2009). In plain language, exhaustion does not just make you tired. It makes you reactive.

This is why the woman who used to laugh off a passive-aggressive email is now drafting three responses and deleting all of them because none felt "professional enough" for what she actually wanted to say. It is why a mildly annoying comment from a coworker can suddenly feel like a personal attack. It is why patience, that thing you used to have in abundance, seems to have quietly left the building sometime around your second missed lunch this week.

None of this means something is wrong with you. It means your brain is running on a system that was built for short bursts of danger, not months of unrelenting demand. Your filter did not disappear because you became a worse person. It went offline because the part of your brain responsible for holding it up is exhausted, too.

This matters because emotional intelligence is often the very thing your career, your relationships, and your leadership depend on. Which means burnout does not just cost you your energy. It costs you the version of yourself who could read a room, absorb feedback without spiraling, and choose her words instead of just releasing them.

The good news is that this is not a character flaw to correct. It is a nervous system to regulate. As the body recovers, so does the filter. Emotional intelligence is not gone. It is buried, and it resurfaces as capacity returns.

When the Body Starts Yelling

Burnout rarely begins with collapse. It begins with subtle signals. You may notice fatigue, difficulty concentrating, irritability, or a sense that everything feels heavier than it should. These early indicators are often dismissed or normalized.

When those signals are ignored, the body escalates. Symptoms become more pronounced, including headaches, muscle tension, disrupted sleep, emotional reactivity, and persistent exhaustion that does not improve with rest. These are not random occurrences. They are communication.

Chronic stress without adequate recovery is associated with disrupted sleep cycles, impaired cognitive functioning, and increased emotional reactivity. Over time, this can create a cycle in which the body is both fatigued and unable to fully rest.

The question becomes not whether your body is speaking, but how long you have been overriding what it has been trying to say. Every override spends capacity you did not know you were spending.

One clarification matters here, and I want to name it directly as a clinician. Everything described in this chapter can be part of the body's response to chronic stress, but many of these same symptoms, persistent fatigue, headaches, sleep disruption, changes in mood, and difficulty concentrating, can also have medical causes that have nothing to do with burnout, from thyroid conditions to anemia to depression. Naming your stress is not a substitute for being checked out. If your symptoms are persistent, worsening, or interfering with your daily life, please see a medical or mental health professional. Listening to your body includes letting a professional help you understand what it is saying.

Your Body Is Not Betraying You

One of the most important reframes in understanding burnout is recognizing that your body is not betraying you. It is protecting you. When you have pushed beyond your capacity for extended periods, your body intervenes. It disrupts your normal functioning because your normal has become unsustainable. This is not sabotage. It is self-preservation. Your body's role is not to maintain your productivity. Its role is to maintain your survival.

Hard Truth

> Your body is not betraying you. It is telling you the truth. Ignore the warning signs long enough, and eventually your body will force you to stop.

The Additional Layer: Stress, Race, and the Body

While burnout affects all women, it is important to acknowledge that stress is not experienced equally. For many Black women, stress includes not only present-day demands but also historical and environmental factors. Research on allostatic load and the weathering hypothesis suggests that chronic exposure to stress, particularly at the intersection of race and gender, is associated with accelerated physiological wear and tear (Geronimus, 1992).

This suggests the body is responding not only to current responsibilities but also to prolonged patterns of strain. Expectations to be strong, to endure, and to persist despite barriers are not isolated experiences. They are shaped by broader cultural and systemic realities.

A Note for Women Living with Grief or Chronic Illness

If your body is also navigating illness, chronic pain, or the weight of significant loss, the physiology described in this chapter is not abstract for you. You are living it in a more immediate and demanding way than most. The allostatic load you carry is real, it is cumulative, and it is not simply the result of pushing too hard. Some of it arrived without your choosing. I want to name that plainly, because too many wellness conversations imply that all depletion is a product of personal choices. Yours is not.

Healing, for you, may move more slowly, require more support, and look different than what this book describes. That is not failure. It is an honest acknowledgment of your reality. You deserve care that meets you there, not where you are expected to be.

The Language of the Body

The body does not communicate in words. It communicates through sensation. Tension, fatigue, irritability, disrupted sleep, and emotional flatness are all forms of communication. Each sensation provides information about what is happening internally. The goal is not to judge these signals, but to listen to them.

Ignoring the body does not eliminate the message. It delays it.

Responding Before the Breakdown

In my work with women navigating burnout, a common reflection is that they did not recognize the severity of their experience until their body forced them to stop. What this often reveals is a pattern of ignoring early signals. However, it does not have to reach that point. It is possible to respond earlier, to notice the subtle shifts, and to make small adjustments before the body escalates its response. This begins with awareness and continues with intentional interruption of patterns.

Monica eventually noticed the pattern in herself, not in one dramatic moment, but in a string of small ones. The snap over the font. The short reply to a friend who didn't deserve it. The tears in the car before she'd even walked into the house. What changed was not that she stopped feeling stretched thin.

What changed was that she started checking in with herself before she reacted, instead of after.

There is a version of you who continues to achieve and show up while also honoring your limits.

That version of you listens sooner, rests without guilt, and responds to the body before it reaches exhaustion. She is not working with more capacity than you have. She is simply reading it honestly, and early.

Chapter Summary

Monica did not snap over a font size. She snapped because she had been overriding her body for months, and it had finally run out of quieter ways to reach her.

1. **Your mind negotiates. Your body reports.** One of them consults your calendar and your sense of what you should be able to handle. The other only tells you what carrying it is actually costing.
2. **Activation was never meant to be permanent.** Your nervous system is built to surge and then recover. Staying in go mode for months is not strength. It is a system that has not been allowed to complete its cycle.
3. **What you do not process, you store.** Suppressed emotion does not disappear. It relocates into the shoulders, the jaw, the chest, and the sleep you are no longer getting.
4. **Burnout costs you your filter, not your character.** The reactivity, the short patience, the reply you would not have sent on a good day: that is an exhausted prefrontal cortex, not a worse version of you.
5. **You learned to stop listening, and it worked.** Every time you overrode a signal and nothing bad happened, the habit got stronger. That is why the disconnection feels like competence rather than loss.
6. **The body is your capacity instrument.** When you stop trusting it, you do not just feel less. You lose the only honest reading you had of how much is left.
7. **You can respond before the escalation.** The signals start quiet. Listening earlier is not indulgence. It is the difference between adjusting and being stopped.

CAPACITY CHECK

Practice This Week

Pause and consider what has come up for you while reading this chapter. This is about recognizing what has already been present. The tension, the fatigue, and the signals your body has been sending are not new. They have likely been there for some time.

The question becomes whether you are ready to listen to them now.

Call to Action: Listen Before It Gets Loud

Choose one moment today to pause and check in with your body. This should not happen at the end of the day when exhaustion has already set in, but during the flow of your day.

Ask yourself what you are feeling and what you need in that moment.

Respond in one small, intentional way. This may include taking a breath, stretching, drinking water, or stepping away briefly. The goal is not to solve everything at once. The goal is to begin listening earlier. The more you respond to your body in quiet moments, the less it will need to raise its voice to be heard.

Body Listening Prompts

If checking in with your body feels unfamiliar, start with these. They are not meant to be answered all at once. Pick one and sit with it for the length of a single breath.

Where in my body am I holding something right now?

What is the first sensation I notice when I stop moving?

When did I last feel genuinely rested, and what was different about that day?

What signal have I been overriding this week?

If my body could say one sentence to me right now, what would it be?

You are not looking for a diagnosis. You are re-establishing contact with the only instrument that can tell you the truth about your capacity.

PHASE III:

THE RESET

Interrupting the Cycle

"Daring to set boundaries is about having the courage to love ourselves even when we risk disappointing others."

~ Brené Brown

Chapter 9

The Power of Boundaries: Breaking the Cycle

"We can't stop others from neglecting us, but we can stop ignoring ourselves."
~ Nedra Glover Tawwab

Linda stared at her phone, her thumb hovering over the screen. The message was simple: "Can you take this on?" She exhaled slowly, already knowing her answer before she gave herself a chance to think about it.

"Yes," she typed, even though her chest tightened as she hit send. Her calendar was already full, her energy was already low, but saying no felt heavier than saying yes.

So she did what she had always done. She made it work.

Later that evening, she sat in silence, exhausted, replaying the moment in her mind. It was not the task itself that overwhelmed her. It was the realization that she had once again chosen obligation over capacity. She had overridden herself without even pausing to ask if she had anything left to give. This is how burnout continues, not just through what you do, but through what you do automatically.

Chapter 3 helped you understand why you push. Chapter 8 showed you how your body responds. This chapter is where the shift begins, and it begins with boundaries. Awareness without interruption keeps you informed, but not transformed. Breaking the cycle of burnout is not about doing less randomly. It is about doing differently, intentionally, and in alignment with your actual capacity. Boundaries are the first tool for that, the way you turn understanding into a different set of choices.

Boundaries Are Not Barriers, They Are Bridges

One of the most misunderstood tools in breaking burnout is boundaries. Many people associate boundaries with rejection, distance, or conflict. In reality, boundaries provide clarity, and that clarity is what teaches people how to treat you.

When I think of boundaries, I think of them as my standards. My personal stop sign. What I am not willing to accept from any of my relationships, whether friends, family, work, or anyone I am in connection with. I also think of a boundary as the protection of my well-being. A boundary helps people begin to respect you differently. It helps them understand what is no longer acceptable.

That is why I have come to think of boundaries as your love letters to yourself. And in those letters, you are teaching people how to understand and treat you differently, because your responses now come from what you have decided you are worth. That reframes boundaries from something that pushes people away into something that lets you stay in connection without abandoning yourself in the process. This is also what makes boundaries a form of burnout prevention. Every limit you hold protects a little more of your capacity, so there is something left at the end of the day that belongs to you.

Without boundaries, everything feels like your responsibility. With boundaries, you begin to discern.

Research supports the importance of this distinction. Studies have shown that individuals who struggle with boundary-setting are more likely to experience emotional exhaustion and burnout because of role overload and lack of control (Maslach & Leiter, 2016).

When expectations are not clearly defined, people tend to overextend themselves in an attempt to meet unspoken demands. Boundaries reduce that ambiguity. They create structure where there was once pressure. They allow you to show up fully without depleting yourself in the process.

And yet, for many high-functioning individuals, boundaries feel uncomfortable, not because they are wrong, but because they are unfamiliar.

The Discomfort of Saying No

Saying no is not always easy. For many, the hesitation is not about the task itself, but about the meaning attached to the decision. Saying no can feel like disappointing someone, letting someone down, or risking how you are perceived. So instead, you say yes, and then you carry the weight of that yes.

Over time, this pattern reinforces the belief that your needs are secondary and that your role is to accommodate, adjust, and absorb. This is especially true for individuals who have been conditioned to be dependable, capable, and strong. However, every yes carries a cost. The question becomes whether you are choosing that cost or defaulting to it. Learning to say no is not about becoming unavailable. It is about becoming intentional and recognizing that your energy is a finite resource, not an unlimited supply.

A few days after that first message, Linda got another one. Different sender, same shape: "Any chance you could jump on this?" She felt the familiar tightening start in her chest, the same one that had shown up right before she typed yes the last time. This time she let her thumb hover a beat longer. She thought about what saying yes would actually cost her that week, not what saying no would look like to the person asking. Then she typed something she had never sent before: "I can't take this on right now, but I can look at it Thursday." She did not apologize for it. She did not add three more sentences to soften it. She sent it, put the phone down, and noticed her chest was still tight. The discomfort had not disappeared. It had just stopped being the deciding vote.

If you need language to borrow while your own is still forming, a boundary can be as simple as: "That does not work for me, but here is what does." "I am not available for that this week." "Let me check my capacity and get back to you tomorrow." "I can help until three, and then I have to go." "I love you, and I cannot take this on." Notice what these sentences have in common. None of them apologizes. None of them over-explains. Each one tells the truth about your capacity and offers only what is actually yours to give. You do not need a perfect script. You need one honest sentence you can deliver without abandoning yourself in the middle of it.

Interrupting Overfunctioning

Overfunctioning is one of the quiet drivers of burnout. It looks like doing more than is required, fixing what is not yours to fix, anticipating needs before they are expressed, and taking responsibility for outcomes that do not belong to you. It is often praised as excellence, reliability, or leadership, but beneath it there is usually something deeper, such as a need for control, fear of failure, an identity built on performance, or self-protection.

Self-determination theory offers one explanation for why this pattern is so persistent. When validation and approval become the primary reward for performance, motivation shifts from something internally driven to something externally controlled, and the behavior becomes harder to interrupt because it is no longer just about the task. It is about maintaining the approval (Deci & Ryan, 2000). The challenge is that this validation can mask depletion. You are praised for what is exhausting you.

Interrupting overfunctioning requires awareness of when you are stepping beyond your role and into over-responsibility. It requires asking different questions, not just "Can I do this?" but "Is this mine to do?" and "What happens if I do not take this on?" Not everything requires your attention or intervention, and not everything benefits from your presence or involvement.

This was the pattern underneath Linda's very first yes, the one at the start of this chapter. She had not paused to ask whether the task was hers to carry. She had answered a question about her capacity with a reflex about her identity. Somewhere along the way, being the one who could be counted on had become inseparable from being worth something. Interrupting that pattern did not require her to become someone who says no to everything. It required her to start asking the question before her thumb moved: is this mine to do?

Slowing Down Is a Skill

Slowing down is often misunderstood as doing less. In reality, it is about doing with intention.

For individuals who have spent years in high-performance mode, slowing down can feel uncomfortable. The absence of urgency can feel like a loss of control, and stillness can feel like inactivity, even when it is necessary.

However, slowing down is not about stopping your life. It is about changing your pace within it.

Research on workplace recovery shows that psychological detachment, the ability to mentally disengage from work during nonwork time, is associated with lower burnout, improved emotional regulation, and better overall well-being (Sonnentag & Fritz, 2015). When the nervous system is given consistent opportunities to return to baseline, it becomes more resilient and less reactive. Slowing down allows your body to catch up with your life. It creates space for reflection, clarity, and decision-making that is not driven by urgency. It also reminds you that your worth is not measured by your speed.

There is a practical version of this, and it is smaller than it sounds. Protect one piece of rest the way you would protect a meeting with someone important. Not the leftover time. Not whatever is still standing at the end of the day. An actual block that exists before anything else gets to claim it.

Most of us treat rest as the thing that happens if there is room. There is never room. Room is not found; it is reserved, and a reservation only holds if you stop offering it to whoever asks next.

Rest that survives only when nothing else needs you is not rest. It is leftovers.

Redefining Capacity

Capacity is not just about time. It includes energy, emotional availability, mental bandwidth, and physical well-being. You may have time to complete a task, but not the capacity to do it well or without consequence to yourself. This is where many people become overwhelmed. They evaluate what they can do based on time rather than on total capacity, leading to overcommitment.

Redefining capacity requires an honest assessment of what you can hold without compromising your well-being. It also requires recognizing that capacity is not fixed. It shifts based on life circumstances, stress levels, and overall health. Research on occupational stress indicates that when individuals consistently operate beyond their capacity, they experience higher levels of burnout, decreased productivity, and reduced effectiveness (Maslach & Leiter, 2016). Doing more does not always lead to better outcomes. Sometimes it leads to a breakdown. Learning your capacity is not limiting; it is protective.

Breaking the Cycle Requires Choice

No single decision created this. A pattern of repeated choices, made automatically and without examination, built this over time. Breaking the cycle is not about one dramatic change, but about consistent, intentional shifts in how you respond to yourself and your environment. It involves choosing to pause before saying yes, asking whether something belongs to you, honoring your limits even when it feels uncomfortable, and redefining success in a way that includes your well-being.

This process is not about perfection. It is about practice. Each time you choose differently, you interrupt the pattern. And interruption is where change begins.

A few weeks later, Linda's phone buzzed with a message that looked almost exactly like the one that opened this chapter. "Can you take this on?" Her chest still tightened. That part had not changed yet, and she was learning it might not for a while. But this time she did not answer before she had asked herself the question. She thought about her calendar, her energy, and what was actually hers to carry. Then she typed: "I can't right now, and that's okay." She did not make it work. She let it be someone else's to figure out. That evening, she sat in silence again, the same way she had at the beginning of this chapter. But this time, the silence did not feel like exhaustion. It felt like room.

One of the greatest misconceptions about boundaries is believing that everyone will understand them, appreciate them, or even agree with them. They won't. For many of us, the discomfort isn't in setting the boundary, it's in managing other people's reactions to it. We fear disappointing people. We fear being misunderstood. We fear being seen as selfish after years of being the dependable one.

This is one of the hardest parts of boundary work, and it is worth saying plainly:

The hardest part of setting a boundary is accepting that some people will not like it, understand it, or agree with it. Once you stop organizing your life around pleasing everyone, holding your own standards gets easier. Not being liked by everyone is a small price to pay for relationships that are actually healthy.

That truth can feel uncomfortable, especially if you've spent much of your life measuring your worth by how available, dependable, or accommodating you've been. But boundaries aren't about controlling other people's reactions. They're about honoring your capacity, protecting your peace, and creating relationships where both people can thrive, not just one.

Hard Truth

Every yes has a price. The only question is who keeps paying it.

CAPACITY CHECK

Choose One Boundary

The patterns you recognized and the moments that felt familiar are not random. They are relevant. It is information.

Consider where in your life you are saying yes when you want to say no.

Reflect on the responsibilities you may be carrying that do not belong to you.

Think about when you tend to overfunction and what may be driving that behavior.

Examine how you currently define your capacity and whether that definition is realistic.

Finally, consider what it would look like to honor your limits without guilt.

Spot Your Over-Functioning Habits

This is not a habit tracker. It is a capacity audit. Read the first column and mark the ones you recognize, then read the second column slowly, because that is the part nobody usually names. Every one of these habits is a withdrawal you have been making without writing it down.

The Habit	What It Currently Costs You	One Interruption to Try
Answering messages the moment they arrive.	Your attention never fully lands on anything, including rest.	Choose two windows a day. Outside them, the message can wait.
Fixing what someone else could have handled.	You spend capacity on work that was never assigned to you, and you teach people to keep assigning it.	Ask: is this mine to do? If the answer is no, let the discomfort sit.
Anticipating needs before they are spoken.	You carry the mental load of other people's planning on top of your own.	Wait to be asked. Being asked is information you have been supplying for free.

Saying yes before checking your week.	You commit capacity you have not counted, then find it by taking it from yourself.	Buy one sentence of time: let me check and get back to you tomorrow.
Redoing work someone else already did.	Two people's capacity spent on one task, and the other person stops trying.	Let it be good enough. Good enough is a real standard, not a failure of one.
Staying available after hours.	Your nervous system never gets the signal that the day ended	Pick a time the day closes. Tell one person about it so it becomes real.

You do not need to interrupt all six. Pick the one whose cost you felt most sharply when you read it. That is the one your capacity is asking you to start with.

Call to Action: One Boundary, One Shift

Today, choose one boundary to set.

It does not have to be big or perfect; it simply needs to be intentional. This may look like saying no to something that does not align with your capacity, pausing before committing, or allowing something to be completed without your involvement.

Between adherence or [illegible] per [illegible]	You commit and you [illegible] take note [illegible] [illegible] yourself.	[illegible] before [illegible] your week.
[illegible]	[illegible]	[illegible]
[illegible]	[illegible]	[illegible]

You don't need to [illegible] [illegible] [illegible] [illegible] when you read [illegible] [illegible]

[illegible]

[illegible] One Boundary, [illegible]

[illegible]

[illegible] [illegible] involvement.

Chapter 10

The S.O.U.L. Framework™

A New Way to Move Through Burnout

"Healing does not begin with a breakthrough. It begins with a breath, a thought, then a decision to move differently."

~ Dr. Tashina Reeder

Renee had done everything right. She had taken the vacation. She had downloaded the meditation app. She had even attended a women's wellness retreat where she cried in a circle of strangers and felt, for about three days afterward, something close to relief. Then Monday came.

The emails returned. The calls resumed. The expectations settled back onto her shoulders like they had never left, and by Wednesday she was already telling herself she would rest again someday. Someday when things slowed down. Someday when she could afford to.

She was not lazy. She was not ungrateful. She was a woman who had done everything the world told her to do to feel better, and she still found herself sitting in the parking lot of her own life, engine off, not ready to go inside. What Renee did not yet understand was that the tools she had been using were not wrong. They were incomplete. She had been treating the symptoms without ever addressing the source. Rest helped, but only until the pattern reasserted itself.

Boundaries felt good until the guilt crept back in. She kept returning to the same place because she kept using short-term strategies to manage a long-term pattern.

That is the gap this chapter is designed to close. By now, you have done significant work. You have seen what burnout looks like from the outside and felt what it does from the inside. You have explored why you push past your limits, what your body has been carrying, and how the cycle sustains itself. You have begun to interrupt patterns and question what has been driving you. That awareness is not small. It is foundational.

But awareness alone is not transformation. Insight without a process is like understanding why you are lost without having a map. You see the problem clearly, you can describe it in detail, and still you do not know which direction to walk. This is where many people get stuck. They understand their burnout intellectually but do not have a structured way to move through it. They read, they reflect, they feel the weight of recognition, and then life speeds back up and the old patterns return by default.

What you need is not just understanding. You need a framework. The S.O.U.L. Framework™ was not created from theory alone. It was developed from lived experience, clinical practice, and years of walking alongside high-achieving women who were tired in ways they could not fully explain. It emerged from my own healing process, from the patterns I observed in my work as a clinician, and from the consistent truth that sustainable change does not happen through willpower. It happens through process.

This framework is your map.

What the S.O.U.L. Framework Is and What It Is Not

The S.O.U.L. Framework™ is a four-phase model for understanding, interrupting, and rebuilding your relationship with yourself, your energy, and your life. It is not a checklist. It is not a shortcut. It is not a program that promises transformation in thirty days if you follow five steps.

It is a process that honors complexity.

The four phases are: Speak Your Truth, Own Your Story, Uplift Your Wellness, and Live in Your Truth. Each phase builds on the one before it. Each one asks something different of you.

Together, they create a pathway from burnout to alignment, not by eliminating ambition, but by grounding it in something sustainable.

Before the four phases get their proper names, it helps to hear them in plainer language, the words women actually use when they describe what changed. Most people do not walk around saying they are in a phase of transformation. They say something quieter.

First comes awareness. *This makes sense now. I can see what is happening.* That is Speak Your Truth, before it has a name: the moment you stop editing your own experience and let it be true.

Then comes understanding. *This makes sense. I know where it came from.* That is Own Your Story: the shift from blaming yourself for the pattern to seeing where the pattern was learned.

Then comes permission. *I am allowed to do this differently.* That is Uplift Your Wellness: the moment caring for yourself stops requiring a justification.

And then comes support. *I do not have to carry this alone.* That is Live in Your Truth: building a life, and a circle, that can hold the weight with you instead of leaving it all on your back.

Awareness. Understanding. Permission. Support. If the four formal names ever feel far away, these four are the same doorway in the words you already use.

S: Speak Your Truth

O: Own Your Story

U: Uplift Your Wellness

L: Live in Your Truth

Before we move into each phase, one important clarification: this is not a linear process.

You will not complete one phase and move permanently to the next. Life is not that orderly. You may find yourself deeply in the Uplift phase and then face a significant life event that calls you back to Speak. You may feel settled in freedom and then encounter a new season that requires you to own something new. The framework is a cycle you will return to as you grow. What changes over time is how quickly you recognize where you are and how skillfully you move through each phase.

Healing is not a destination. It is a direction.

S: Speak Your Truth: The Power of Transparency

The first phase sounds simple. It is not. Speak Your Truth is the practice of honest acknowledgment. It is naming what is actually happening, not the version of events you have edited for others, not the answer that keeps the peace, not the story that makes your exhaustion sound acceptable. It is the truth you tell yourself when no one is listening.

For many high-achieving women, this is the most difficult phase because it requires lowering a defense that has served them well for a long time. When you have spent years being the capable one, the dependable one, the one who handles things, honesty can feel like exposure.

Saying "I am not okay" can feel like losing ground. Admitting that something is wrong can feel like giving someone permission to doubt you.

But silence is not protection. It is prolonged suffering. Shame researcher Brené Brown has written extensively on the relationship between secrecy and shame, describing how shame grows in silence and loses its power when it is brought into the light of honest language (Brown, 2012). When you cannot name what you are experiencing, you cannot begin to address it. When you normalize exhaustion, you extend it. When you perform wellness while privately unraveling, you widen the distance between who you are performing to be and who you actually are. That distance is costly.

It is one of the most invisible sources of fatigue. Speaking your truth does not require an audience. It does not mean telling everyone everything. It means allowing yourself to be honest about your internal experience without immediately dismissing it, minimizing it, or burying it under productivity.

What This Phase Looks Like in Practice

Renee's version of this phase looked like a moment in her car, the same parking lot she had been sitting in for months, when she finally stopped talking herself out of what she felt. She put her hand over her chest, took a breath, and said out loud to no one: "I am exhausted. I am sad. And I do not know how much longer I can keep doing this." Nothing changed immediately. The job was still there. The emails were still waiting. But something shifted internally the moment she stopped arguing against her own experience. That acknowledgment created a small but significant opening.

Your version of this phase might look like journaling without censoring yourself. It might look like telling a trusted person the honest version instead of the managed version. It might look like pausing in the middle of a full day and asking: "How am I actually doing right now?" Not the rehearsed answer. Not the socially acceptable one. The real one.

You cannot shift what you have not named, and you cannot protect a capacity you will not admit has limits.

Transparency is not weakness. It is the first act of healing.

O: Own Your Story: Understanding the Root

Once you have spoken the truth about your experience, the next phase asks you to go deeper. Not just what you are feeling, but why. Not just the symptoms, but the source.

Owning your story is the process of understanding how your history, your conditioning, and the patterns you developed to survive have shaped how you show up in the world today. This is not about blame. It is not about excavating every painful memory or re-opening wounds that do not need to be disturbed. It is about developing enough insight into your own patterns that you can see them clearly, understand them compassionately, and begin to choose differently. Many high-achieving behaviors are not simply ambition. As discussed in Chapter 3, research in trauma psychology indicates that performance-based identities are frequently rooted in environments where safety, belonging, or approval felt conditional. When children grow up learning that love is connected to achievement, or that needing anything makes them unsafe, they develop strategies to protect themselves. Those strategies become identity. Over time, you stop seeing them as adaptations and start experiencing them as simply "who you are" (LePera, 2021).

Owning your story means examining those adaptations with curiosity rather than judgment.

It means asking: Where did I first learn that I had to earn rest? Where did I learn that needing help was unsafe? Whose voice is it that tells me I am not doing enough? What was I protecting myself from when I first developed the habit of overextending? These questions are not meant to produce paralysis. They are meant to produce insight. And insight is what creates the distance between stimulus and response, the small but crucial space where choice becomes possible.

What This Phase Looks Like in Practice

Renee's version of this phase started with a question she almost didn't let herself finish: why does rest feel like something I have to earn? The answer, when she sat with it, went back further than her calendar. She had grown up watching a parent whose worth seemed to rise and fall with how much they got done in a day. Stillness in that house had never looked safe. It looked like something was wrong. She had not consciously decided that busyness equaled safety. She had absorbed it, the way children absorb the emotional weather of a house long before they understand it. What she had been calling ambition was, underneath it, a much older strategy for staying okay.

What she carries into adulthood is the belief that stillness equals danger, that stopping means something will fall apart, and that her worth is directly proportional to what she can manage. She does not experience this as a survival strategy. She experiences it as her personality.

She calls it discipline. She calls it ambition. And she wonders why rest feels so threatening.

Owning her story would mean recognizing that connection and extending compassion to the version of herself who needed it. It is not about pathologizing her drive. It is about understanding where it came from so she can decide what she wants to carry forward.

What was learned can be unlearned. What protected you then does not have to control you now.

U: Uplift Your Wellness: Healing the Whole Person

The third phase is where healing moves from internal understanding into embodied practice. Uplifting your wellness is not about optimizing yourself into a more efficient machine. It is about restoring the capacity that burnout spent, and then learning to live within it rather than constantly past it.

Wellness, in this framework, is not a destination or a lifestyle aesthetic. It is not green juice and gratitude journals if those things do not genuinely serve you. It is the intentional practice of attending to your whole self in ways that are honest, sustainable, and aligned with your actual needs. And because burnout affects people across multiple dimensions simultaneously, wellness must also be approached holistically.

Emotional wellness involves developing the capacity to recognize, process, and express your emotions without being overwhelmed by them or suppressing them entirely. It includes learning to grieve what needs grieving, to feel anger without acting destructively on it, and to experience joy without immediately reaching for the next obligation. As discussed in Chapter 8, unprocessed emotions are not neutral. They take up residence in the body and contribute to the physical symptoms of burnout. Emotional wellness is not softness. It is load management.

Mental wellness involves interrupting the cognitive patterns that sustain burnout, including perfectionism, catastrophic thinking, and the relentless internal commentary that tells you that what you are doing is never enough. It includes rest for the mind, not just for the body.

Sleep is not the only form of mental recovery. Silence, creative play, and freedom from constant problem-solving are all forms of mental rest that many high-achieving women have stopped giving themselves permission to access. Physical wellness involves listening to your body as a source of information rather than an obstacle to your productivity. It involves nourishment, movement, sleep, and medical attention that is not deferred until crisis. Many of the women I work with have developed a habit of ignoring physical signals until those signals become emergencies. Your body is not a machine to be maintained. It is a living system that reflects the cumulative weight of everything you have been carrying.

Spiritual wellness, as I use it here, is inclusive. Whether your spirituality is rooted in faith, in nature, in community, or in a deep sense of personal purpose, this dimension of wellness speaks to the need for meaning. Burnout is not only about doing too much. It is also about feeling disconnected from why you are doing it. When your daily life feels increasingly distant from your deepest values, spiritual depletion sets in alongside the physical and emotional.

Reconnecting to purpose, even in small ways, is restorative in ways that no productivity strategy can replace.

What This Phase Looks Like in Practice

For Renee, uplifting her wellness did not begin with a sweeping life overhaul. It began with one decision she made on a Tuesday afternoon when a colleague asked her to take on an additional project. For the first time, she paused before answering. She thought about her actual capacity. She thought about what saying yes would cost her that week, that month, in terms of the energy she had been trying to rebuild. And she said, calmly and without extensive explanation: "I do not have the bandwidth for that right now, but I am glad to revisit it next quarter." That was it. No grand announcement. No lengthy boundary conversation. One decision, made from awareness rather than habit.

It was uncomfortable. She spent part of that afternoon second-guessing herself. But her body did not tighten the way it usually did when she overcommitted. Something felt different.

Not perfect. Not resolved. Different. Wellness is built in moments like that. Accumulated over time, those moments become a different way of living.

Research supports this incremental approach. Research on habit formation shows that small, consistent changes tend to be more sustainable over time than dramatic interventions, because behaviors repeated in stable contexts gradually become automatic rather than effortful (Wood & Neal, 2007). Your body does not need a complete life overhaul.

It needs consistent signals that things are changing. Each time you respond to your own needs before you override them, you send that signal.

L: Live in Your Truth: Rebuilding in Alignment

The final phase is not a finish line. It is a way of being.

Living in Your Truth means telling yourself the truth so consistently that it becomes the ground you stand on. It is that ground, not constant vigilance, that lets you live freely, without performing a version of yourself that isn't real.

Living in your truth does not mean the absence of difficulty, pressure, or responsibility. It does not mean you will never feel tired or never face seasons that stretch you. Living in your truth is freedom. Freedom, in this framework, means that you are no longer operating from survival. You are no longer driven by fear of not being enough, or by the belief that slowing down will somehow undermine your progress. You move through your life from a place of alignment, making choices that reflect your values rather than simply responding to external demands.

This phase is where the earlier work becomes your new foundation. You have spoken the truth about your experience. You have owned the patterns that brought you here. You have begun uplifting your wellness in ways that are honest and sustainable. Now you integrate all of that into the inner workings of your daily life.

Living in freedom looks like making decisions from capacity rather than obligation. It looks like success that includes your well-being in the definition. It looks like ambition that does not require you to abandon yourself in the process of achieving it. It looks like a life that, even in its full and demanding seasons, does not require constant recovery from itself.

Self-determination theory, developed by Ryan and Deci (2017), identifies three core psychological needs that must be met for genuine well-being: autonomy, competence, and relatedness. The next chapter explores each of these needs in depth.

Burnout systematically erodes all three. Living in your truth is the practice of restoring all three.

What This Phase Looks Like in Practice

Freedom is not a single dramatic moment of liberation. For most women, it arrives quietly, in ordinary situations that once would have depleted them but now feel different.

It looked like Renee, months later, sitting in that same parking lot after work, realizing she was not dreading walking inside. The work is still hard. The demands are still real.

But she is no longer carrying the weight of a self she has been performing. She knows her limits, and she respects them. She knows her values, and she makes decisions that reflect them. She knows when she is approaching her edge, and she responds before she reaches exhaustion.

She is not perfect. She still has days when the old patterns pull. But she has a process now. She knows how to come back to herself.

That is what freedom looks like. Not the absence of struggle, but the presence of something solid to return to.

For you, freedom may look like restructuring your schedule to include genuine recovery time without guilt. It may look like releasing the version of success that required constant sacrifice and building one that includes your peace. It may look like pursuing your goals with the same energy and drive, but from a place of purpose rather than fear. It may look like finally allowing yourself to be known, not just admired.

Hard Truth

Understanding why you're experiencing burnout can give you insight, but insight alone will not heal you. Healing happens when you choose differently, over and over, until a new way of living becomes your own.

The Framework in Motion

The S.O.U.L. Framework is not a one-time process. It is a cycle you will return to as your life evolves. There will be seasons when your capacity expands and seasons when it contracts, and the framework meets you in both. There will be times when you move through all four phases in a single hard week, and times when one phase holds you for a year.

This is not failure. This is growth.

Each time you move through the framework, you do so with more awareness, more skill, and more compassion for yourself than you had before. The goal is not to reach a point where you never experience burnout again. The goal is to develop such an intimate knowledge of your own patterns that you recognize the early signals, respond before they escalate, and trust yourself to know what you need.

You have arrived at this chapter having already done the work of Phases I, II, and III in this book. You have seen what you have been carrying. You have examined why you keep going. You have begun to interrupt the cycle. The S.O.U.L. Framework™ is not separate from that work. It is the playbook that holds all of it together.

Every chapter you have read lives within this framework. The Speak work runs through Phase I, where you first began naming what burnout looks like and feels like. The Own work anchors Phase II, where you examined why you push past your limits and where burnout originates. The Uplift work belongs to Phase III, where you began interrupting the cycle and restoring what had been depleted. And the chapters ahead, in Phase IV, belong to Live. You have already been working within this model. Now you have language for the full map.

That is what the framework protects: the small, repeatable moments (a breath, a thought, a decision to move differently) and the structure that turns them into a life.

CAPACITY CHECK

Locate Yourself in the Framework

Each of the four phases asks something specific of you. You may be in one phase predominantly right now, or you may recognize yourself across all four. This is not a test. It is an inventory, an honest accounting of where you are so you can know what you need next.

Where Are You in the S.O.U.L. Framework?

Read through each phase below. As you read, notice which description feels most like your current experience. There are no right or wrong answers. Most people move through these phases gradually and may even see themselves in more than one. Simply choose the phase that best describes where you are today.

S: Speak

You're beginning to acknowledge your burnout.

You may be in the Speak phase if:

You struggle to name what is really happening.

You minimize your exhaustion or convince yourself you're "just tired."

You work hard to manage what others see while hiding how overwhelmed you feel.

Being transparent feels uncomfortable or even unsafe.

Saying "I'm not okay" still feels impossible, or is quickly followed by "but I'm fine."

Reflection: Am I giving myself permission to tell the truth about what I'm carrying?

O: Own

You're beginning to understand your patterns.

You may be in the Own phase if:

You recognize your burnout patterns but are still trying to understand where they came from.

You often ask yourself: Why do I keep pushing myself? Why is rest so difficult? Why does other people's approval matter so much?

You're beginning to connect your past experiences with your present behaviors.

You know your patterns, but you're still learning how to change them.

Reflection: What old belief or experience continues to shape how I live today?

U: Uplift

You're building new habits, but consistency is still a challenge.

You may be in the Uplift phase if:

You know what you need but struggle to consistently give it to yourself.

Your boundaries are becoming clearer, but maintaining them still feels uncomfortable.

You're practicing healthier habits, yet they haven't become your normal way of living.

You experience progress, followed by periods of slipping back into old patterns.

Reflection: What one practice would help me honor my capacity more consistently?

L: Live

You're living from alignment instead of survival.

You may be in the Live phase if:

You make decisions that reflect your values instead of other people's expectations.

You honor your capacity without constant guilt.

You pursue your purpose without continually abandoning yourself.

Rest, boundaries, and self-care have become part of your lifestyle, not just your recovery.

Freedom feels less like a goal and more like the way you're learning to live, even if imperfectly.

Reflection: How has my life changed because I chose to honor my well-being?

Apply the S.O.U.L. Framework™

Call to Action: Choose Your Entry Point

You do not need to begin at the beginning. You need to begin where you are.

Review the four phases and identify the one that most honestly reflects your current experience.

If you are in Speak:

Write one true sentence about how you are actually feeling. Do not edit it. Do not justify it. Just let it be true.

If you are in Own:

Identify one belief about your worth that is not yours to carry. Write where it came from and what it has cost you.

If you are in Uplift:

Choose one area of your wellness that has been neglected and take one concrete, specific action to begin restoring it this week.

If you are in Live:

Celebrate your progress. Write a letter to the version of yourself who first entered the Speak phase. Tell them what has changed, what you've learned, and why choosing yourself was worth it. Then identify one daily practice you will continue to protect so that the life you've built remains aligned with your values and capacity.

PHASE IV:

THE INTEGRATION AND REBUILD

Creating a Life That Supports You

"Your focus should not be on
who you were but rather the pursuit of who you can become."
~ Sarah Jakes Roberts, Woman Evolve

Chapter 11

Reconnecting With Yourself: Emotional Awareness, Identity, and Rest

"You may not control all the events that happen to you,
but you can decide not to be reduced by them."
~ Dr. Maya Angelou, Letter to My Daughter

Alicia sat in the corner of her quiet living room, her laptop closed for once, her phone turned face down beside her. There was nothing urgent pulling at her, no deadlines pressing against her chest, no one asking her for anything. She had the evening entirely to herself, something she had been telling herself she wanted for months. And now that it was here, she did not know what to do with it.

She tried reading. She put the book down after two pages. She thought about calling a friend, but the idea of performing wellness over the phone felt exhausting. She opened the refrigerator twice without taking anything out. She sat back down on the couch, and in the silence, something uncomfortable surfaced. Not a thought exactly. More like a question. Who am I when I am not doing anything?

She could not answer it. Not because she lacked intelligence or self-awareness. But because for as long as she could remember, she had known herself through motion. Through the titles she carried, the problems she solved, the expectations she met. Stillness was not a place she recognized. It was a place she had always moved through quickly on the way to the next thing.

That evening, Alicia did not have a breakthrough. She did not suddenly discover herself or feel a wave of peace wash over her. What she had, for the first time in a long time, was an honest encounter with how far she had drifted from herself. And that encounter, uncomfortable as it was, was the beginning.

This is where burnout often deposits you. Not with a dramatic collapse or a clear moment of crisis, but with a quiet, disorienting unfamiliarity with your own interior life. You have been so busy holding everything together, producing, performing, showing up, that the version of you who exists beneath all of that has grown distant. And now, in the stillness that recovery requires, you realize you do not quite know her anymore. This chapter is about finding your way back.

Reconnecting with yourself is not a luxury or a bonus step in the recovery process. It is the foundation upon which everything else depends. You cannot honor a capacity you have lost contact with, and you cannot protect a self you no longer recognize. Recovery that skips this step rebuilds the output and leaves the person underneath it exactly as depleted as before.

Emotional Awareness: Listening Without Judgment

The first step in reconnecting with yourself is developing the capacity to recognize what you are actually feeling, without immediately doing something about it.

This sounds simpler than it is. Most high-achieving women have become highly skilled at emotional management, which is not the same as emotional awareness. Management means keeping feelings contained, functional, and out of the way so that you can continue performing. Awareness means pausing to notice what is present, naming it accurately, and allowing it to exist without immediately being redirected.

The distinction matters because managed emotions do not go away. As discussed in Chapter 8, research in psychophysiology has found that emotional suppression is associated with increased physiological stress responses, including elevated heart rate, muscle tension, and prolonged nervous system activation (Gross & Levenson, 1997). When emotions are consistently redirected rather than processed, they accumulate. They show up in the body. They surface as irritability, numbness, or the vague but persistent sense that something is wrong without a clear explanation.

Psychologist James Gross, whose work on emotional regulation has been foundational in the field, distinguished between antecedent-focused regulation, which involves shaping how you think about a situation before you respond, and response-focused regulation, which involves suppressing or overriding a feeling after it has already arisen (Gross, 1998). Most burned-out high achievers tend toward the second kind. They feel the exhaustion, the resentment, the grief, and they override it. They function. And the cost accumulates beneath the surface.

Emotional awareness is the practice of interrupting that cycle at its origin. It is learning to ask: What am I actually feeling right now? And then staying with the answer long enough to let it be informative rather than threatening. For Alicia, this looked unglamorous. It looked like sitting on her couch with an unread book beside her, noticing a tightness in her chest she could not explain, and resisting the urge to pick up her phone and fill the silence. It looked like acknowledging, without trying to fix it, that what she felt was something close to grief. Not grief for a specific loss, but grief for all the evenings she had not allowed herself to simply exist in.

That is where emotional awareness begins. Not in a therapist's office, not in a structured exercise, but in the ordinary moments when you choose to stay present with what you feel rather than moving past it. You are not behind on your emotions. You are catching up to them. And that is not a weakness.

That is the beginning of honesty.

Developing emotional awareness is also a skill that deepens over time. Research by Lisa Feldman Barrett on emotional granularity, the ability to distinguish between different emotional states with precision, suggests that people who have a more nuanced emotional vocabulary tend to experience less emotional reactivity and greater psychological resilience (Barrett, 2017). This means that learning to differentiate between anxious and overwhelmed, between disappointed and ashamed, between tired and grieving, is not merely academic. It is practically protective. The more accurately you can name what you are experiencing, the more effectively you can respond to it. You do not have to have the right words immediately. What matters is the willingness to stay with the question long enough for an honest answer to arrive.

Let me tell you what this looks like in my own life, because I do not want it to stay theoretical. I do a check-in with myself, on purpose. I ask three questions. How is my relationship with God? How is my relationship with the people around me? And, most important, how is my relationship with myself? Then one more: what do I actually need in this moment? I tell my clients to do the same thing, not once, but throughout the day, especially when their mood shifts. Because it will shift. Things happen between morning and night, and your body keeps score of all of it.

So, when you notice you are suddenly tired, or annoyed, or dreading the thing you were fine about an hour ago, that is the signal. That is your body telling you something changed. The whole skill is learning to stop and ask what, instead of pushing past it and paying for it later. That is what awareness actually is. Not a feeling you wait for. A question you are willing to ask yourself, honestly, again and again.

Identity Beyond Performance

Alicia's question, who am I when I am not performing, is not a question with a quick answer. It is the central question of this chapter, and it is one that burnout forces to the surface whether you are ready for it or not. For many high-achieving women, identity has been constructed almost entirely around function.

You are a clinician, a founder, a mother, a leader, a provider, a problem-solver. These are not small things. They are meaningful. But when they become the totality of how you understand yourself, you have created an identity that is entirely dependent on output. An identity that can only exist when it is being used.

The psychological term for this is contingent self-worth, a construct developed by Jennifer Crocker and Lora Park in their research on the costs of pursuing self-esteem through external achievement. Their findings showed that individuals whose self-worth is heavily contingent on performance, approval, or success experience greater anxiety, more volatile emotional states, and lower long-term well-being than those with a more stable, internally grounded self-concept (Crocker & Park, 2004). They also found that the pursuit of external validation, even when successful, does not satisfy the underlying need. It simply defers the question.

That is the trap. You achieve, and it feels good briefly, and then the standard moves, and you have to achieve again to maintain the same sense of worth. There is no arrival point. There is only the next proof of adequacy.

Burnout often breaks this cycle not because it heals the underlying pattern, but because it removes the capacity to keep performing. When the output stops, whether by force of exhaustion or necessity, the identity built on that output destabilizes. This is why rest can feel so threatening. It is not just physical discomfort. It is an identity disruption. When you stop doing, you come face to face with the question of who you are without it.

Reconnecting with yourself means expanding your sense of identity to include your values, your inner life, your relationships, your curiosity, your history, your faith, your humor, your grief, and your longing. It means building a self that does not disappear when the titles are removed.

Self-determination theory, developed by Ryan and Deci, identifies three core psychological needs that are fundamental to well-being regardless of achievement level: autonomy, competence, and relatedness. Autonomy is not independence from others but the sense that your actions align with your genuine values rather than external pressure. Competence is not performance but the felt sense that you are effective in ways that matter to you. Relatedness is connection, the experience of being known and valued for who you are, not only for what you deliver (Ryan & Deci, 2017). Burnout erodes all three. Reconnection begins to restore them.

Alicia began this process slowly and imperfectly. She started asking herself, in small moments, what she actually enjoyed, not what she was good at or what was expected, but what she genuinely liked. She found, to her mild embarrassment, that she liked cooking elaborate meals when no one was watching. That she liked old photographs. That she had opinions about architecture. None of it was dramatic. But it was hers, and that felt significant.

You are not only what you produce.

You are not only what you can hold together.

You were someone before you learned to perform, and that person has been waiting patiently for you to come back.

There is a permission most of us were never given, and never thought to give ourselves. The permission to be a whole person rather than a useful one.

You are allowed to have needs that inconvenience other people. You are allowed to want things that do not produce anything. You are allowed to rest, to take up space, to be loved for who you are rather than what you can provide. None of that has to be deserved first. It was always yours.

You do not have to be useful to be worthy of the capacity you were born with.

Relearning Rest

Rest should be common sense. It is not.

For women who have built their identity around output, rest is rarely experienced as neutral. It carries a weight of meaning that goes well beyond relaxation. Rest can feel like falling behind. Like being irresponsible. Like choosing yourself at the expense of someone who is depending on you. For some, rest triggers anxiety that makes it nearly impossible to enjoy, because the mind remains active even when the body is still, pondering the unfinished tasks, the expectations that are not being met, the proof of worth that is not being accumulated.

In Chapter 8, this was named in passing: rest anxiety, the particular discomfort of finally getting the stillness your body has been asking for and being unable to settle into it. This is the chapter where we stay with it, because for many high-achieving women, learning to rest is not a scheduling problem. It is a nervous-system problem.

If you have felt it, you know the shape of it. You sit down, and a voice starts up. Listen to what it actually says.

You should be doing something.

This is a waste of time.

You will pay for this later.

Other people are getting ahead while you sit here.

That voice is not the truth. It is the sound of a nervous system that has been rewarded for vigilance for so long that safety now registers as danger. When rest finally arrives, the body does not relax. It braces, because slowing down is the one thing it was trained to treat as a threat.

I had to make peace with silence before I could rest in it. For a long time, quiet made me uneasy, so I filled it. Now I protect it. I silence my phone. Sometimes I tag out from social media completely, which, if you are an entrepreneur, sounds counterproductive, because we are told visibility is gold. It is how you make your money. People have to see you to build that like-know-trust factor, so you stay visible, and it is a lot. But sometimes I needed the peace more than I needed to be seen. So, I built quiet on purpose. No television, no phone, no scrolling. Just me and a book. Sometimes just me and some music. Sometimes me and my devotionals, or worship playing low while I let my mind settle and get grounded again. None of that is impressive. Nobody claps for it. But it is some of the most restorative work I do, and it is where a lot of my peace actually comes from.

Rest anxiety is not proof that you cannot rest. It is proof of how long you went without it. This is not a character flaw. It is a conditioned response. And like all conditioned responses, it can be retrained.

The first thing to understand about rest is its scope. Rest is not simply the absence of work. Physician Saundra Dalton-Smith, in her work on the seven types of rest, describes rest as spanning multiple distinct dimensions, each addressing a different aspect of human functioning (Dalton-Smith, 2017). Physical rest includes both passive rest, such as sleep, and active rest, such as gentle movement or stretching that releases tension.

Mental rest involves reducing cognitive load, stepping away from problem-solving, and allowing the mind to wander without agenda. Sensory rest involves stepping back from the constant input of screens, notifications, and noise, giving your senses a genuine break from stimulation. Creative rest is the replenishment that comes from experiencing beauty and inspiration, whether in nature, art, or music, without being required to produce anything in response.

Emotional rest is the experience of being in spaces or relationships where you do not have to manage how you are perceived, where you can simply be without performance. Social rest is the relief that comes from time alone or from interactions that are genuinely restorative rather than draining. Spiritual rest involves connection to meaning, to community, to faith, or to the sense that your life has purpose beyond your productivity.

Most people, when they finally allow themselves to rest, access only the physical dimension. They sleep. And then they wonder why they still feel depleted. It is because the emotional, mental, and spiritual deficits have not been addressed. You can sleep ten hours and wake up exhausted if you have been running on empty.

This is also why rest does not always have to mean sleep. A change of scenery, as small as it sounds, can deliver several of those other dimensions at once. Stepping outside gives your senses a break from screens and noise. Moving to a different room quiets the mental load of the space you were grinding in. A few minutes near something beautiful, a window, a tree, the sky, offer a small dose of the creative and even spiritual rest that sitting at your desk never will. I say this often, because I believe it: a change of scenery does the heart and the soul well. When your mind is tired, and your nervous system is dysregulated, moving your body into a different environment can give you the second breath of air you did not know you needed.

This matters especially when sleep is not available, when you are in the middle of the workday and lying down is not an option. You can still move to a different room, sit near a window, or walk to the end of the block. Part of relearning rest is recognizing that a resting state can be achieved in more than one way, and that you do not always have to wait until bedtime to give your body what it needs.

Relearning rest also means confronting the internalized voice that says rest must be earned. For many women, this voice is loud and specific. It sounds like the people who first taught them that stillness was laziness. It sounds like the workplace culture that praised overwork. It sounds like the version of success they absorbed before they were old enough to question it. Recognizing that voice as learned, rather than true, is not a small thing. It is one of the primary cognitive shifts that makes genuine rest possible.

Research on recovery from occupational stress highlights the importance of what psychologists call psychological detachment, the ability to mentally disengage from work during non-work hours, a skill you first met in Chapter 9. Studies show that individuals who can genuinely detach during recovery periods experience lower fatigue, higher well-being, and greater engagement when they return to work, compared to those who remain cognitively connected to work obligations during rest (Sonnentag & Bayer, 2005).

Psychological detachment is not about being uninvested in your work. It is about having a self that exists and is valued outside of it.

Alicia's first attempt at genuine rest looked like failure. She sat in the garden on a Saturday morning with coffee and nothing else, and lasted eleven minutes before she brought her phone outside. The second Saturday, she lasted twenty. By the fourth, something shifted. The silence stopped feeling like a warning and started feeling like a space she could actually breathe in. Not peace, not yet. But something less like a threat. That was enough to keep going.

Rest is a skill you rebuild slowly. The nervous system needs repeated evidence that slowing down is safe before it will fully allow it. You are not doing it wrong if it feels uncomfortable at first. You are doing exactly what the work requires.

Nervous System Regulation: Returning to Safety

Everything discussed in this chapter, emotional awareness, identity expansion, relearning rest, connects to a physiological reality that cannot be bypassed through willpower alone. After extended periods of burnout, your nervous system has adapted to function in a state of chronic activation. Meaning, you are always "on." It has learned that high alertness is the default. And because nervous systems learn through repetition, the transition out of that state requires more than a single weekend of rest or a decision to slow down. It requires consistent, repeated experiences of safety.

The autonomic nervous system operates along a spectrum. At one end is sympathetic activation, the fight-or-flight state that mobilizes the body for perceived threat, increasing heart rate, sharpening focus, elevating cortisol and adrenaline. At the other end is parasympathetic activation, the rest-and-digest state where the body repairs, digests, consolidates memory, and restores. As discussed in Chapter 8, chronic stress keeps the body tilted toward the sympathetic end of that spectrum, which means that even in objectively safe and quiet moments, the body may continue to generate urgency signals.

Polyvagal theory, an evolutionary framework developed by neuroscientist Stephen Porges, offers one useful lens for understanding this dynamic. Porges proposes what he calls the ventral vagal state, associated with social engagement, as the physiological condition in which humans feel safe, connected, and capable of rest and creativity. In his theory, prolonged stress and trauma can dysregulate this system, shifting people into defensive states, fight-flight or freeze, that come to feel normal because they have been the dominant experience for so long (Porges, 2011). While polyvagal theory is one framework among several and aspects of it continue to be debated among researchers, its central invitation is echoed across the wider stress literature: returning to regulation is not only psychological. It is a physiological process that involves the body receiving repeated signals that the threat has passed.

This is why practices that engage the body directly are not supplementary to recovery. They are foundational. Deep, slow breathing helps activate the vagus nerve and shift the autonomic balance toward parasympathetic dominance. Gentle movement releases stored tension and helps metabolize stress hormones. Grounding practices, such as feeling your feet on the floor or holding something with texture and weight, signal presence to a nervous system that has been living in anticipation. Warmth, whether a bath, a cup of tea, or sunlight on skin, is neurologically associated with safety. Consistent sleep rhythms help recalibrate the circadian cycle that chronic stress disrupts.

These are not soft suggestions. They are grounded, evidence-informed ways of supporting a dysregulated nervous system. Research consistently indicates that somatic practices targeting the autonomic nervous system are associated with measurable improvements in anxiety, emotional regulation, and burnout recovery (McEwen, 2007; van der Kolk, 2014).

For Alicia, regulation began with something she had not done in years: she started taking walks without her phone. Not long walks. Fifteen minutes, sometimes less. But walks taken slowly, with her attention on what was around her rather than inside her head. Over weeks, she noticed that she returned from those walks slightly different. Less reactive. More present. Something in her body was beginning to remember that stillness was not danger.

Your nervous system does not need a retreat. It needs repetition. Small, consistent signals of safety, offered over time, become the ground that a restored capacity can actually stand on. You are not looking for one big recovery. You are teaching your body that having something left is okay.

Reconnection as a Lifelong Practice

It is important to say clearly that reconnection with yourself is not an event. It is not a moment of clarity that arrives and then stays permanently. It is a practice, and like all practices, it must be returned to. Life will continue to make demands. Seasons will arise that require more of you than you planned to give. There will be periods when you drift again, when the distance between who you are performing to be and who you actually are begins to widen without your noticing.

What changes over time is not that the drift stops happening. What changes is how quickly you recognize it, and how skilled you become at finding your way back.

It helps to know what the shift actually feels like, because it is quiet enough to miss. You will not wake up one morning reconnected. What you will notice, eventually, is smaller and more reliable than that. You catch the drift sooner. You feel the tightening in your chest and you recognize it this time. You hear the voice telling you to override yourself and, for once, you pause before you obey it.

The healing is not that you stopped being on autopilot. It is that you learned how to find your way back and how much faster you can do it now.

This chapter introduced four practices: emotional awareness, identity beyond performance, relearning rest, and nervous system regulation. None of them are things you master once. They are commitments you renew. Some days that will feel meaningful and grounding. Some days it will feel mechanical. Both are fine. Consistency matters more than inspiration.

Alicia did not resolve her question that first evening. But she kept sitting with it. She kept showing up to the silence. And slowly, over months, she began to recognize something in the quiet that felt like herself. Not the self she performed. Not the self she had trained to be capable and contained. Something older and quieter and more honest than either of those.

That is what this chapter is an invitation to. Not a transformation that happens all at once, but a gradual, faithful return to the person who was always there, waiting for you to stop long enough to meet her again.

Hard Truth

> You are meeting yourself again.
> Not the woman everyone needed.
> Not the woman who kept proving herself.
> The woman underneath all of it.
> She's been waiting for you.

CAPACITY CHECK

Reconnect With Yourself

Take your time here. This chapter asked something deeper than practical shifts or new habits. It asked you to consider the relationship you have with yourself, and that deserves honest reflection rather than a quick scan.

Reconnection is not renovation.

You are not building a brand-new version of yourself. You are unlearning the beliefs, behaviors, and internal narratives that taught you to live beyond your capacity. Many of those beliefs were shaped by life experiences and the meaning you attached to them. They may have helped you survive one season of your life, but they were never meant to lead the rest of your life.

Reconnection is learning to replace those old narratives with healthier ones that honor your worth, protect your peace, and allow you to live within your capacity. That kind of change takes time. It takes patience. And it takes the willingness to stay present with what you discover along the way.

Journaling Prompts

When I am not doing anything, I feel...

The emotion I have been managing around most lately is...

I stopped knowing myself when...

The version of me that existed before the performing, the producing, and the holding it together liked...

One small signal of safety I can give my nervous system today is...

Chapter 12

Redefining Success: Where Wellness, Peace, Purpose, and Ambition Coexist

"Success isn't about how much money you make.
It's about the difference you make in people's lives."
~ Michelle Obama

Mary had achieved everything she once set out to accomplish.

The career she had mapped out at twenty-three was now her reality at forty-one. Senior director. Six-figure income. A name people recognized in her field. She had the house, the credentials, the LinkedIn profile that made former classmates pause. She had, by every measure she had inherited, made it.

And yet, sitting at her desk on a Tuesday evening long after her team had gone home, the screen's glow falling across a face that had not smiled easily in months, she felt the particular hollowness of a woman who had won a race she no longer believed in.

She tried to locate the satisfaction. She looked for it the way you search for a word that sits just at the edge of memory. She knew it had been there once. Early in her career, when each promotion felt like confirmation that the work mattered. When staying late felt like an investment rather than a habit. When the recognition meant something because she still knew what she was trying to prove.

But somewhere in the accumulation of achievements, the goalposts had kept moving, the wins had gotten smaller in feeling even as they grew larger on paper, and Mary had stopped asking whether any of it was actually what she wanted. She had been too busy achieving to notice that achieving had become the point itself. A means that had quietly replaced its own end.

That Tuesday evening, she did not resign. She did not have a crisis. She simply sat with a question she had been outrunning for years, one that had been waiting patiently at the finish line of every goal she had crossed.

Is this what I was building toward? Because if it is, why doesn't it feel like enough?

That question is not a sign that something is wrong with Mary. It is a sign that something is finally honest.

Burnout does not only challenge your capacity; it challenges your definitions. When exhaustion strips away the ability to simply keep pushing, what is left is the opportunity, often uncomfortable, sometimes unwanted, to examine what you have been pushing toward and whether it still deserves that much of you. A definition of success that requires more than you have to give is not a high standard. It is a slow way of running out.

This chapter is about that examination. Not to dismantle your ambition or convince you to want less. But to invite you to want more honestly, to build toward something that includes you in the vision of success rather than requiring you to disappear inside it.

The redefinition this chapter asks for does not run in the direction you might expect. It is not about achieving more, and it is not about achieving less. It is about a different axis altogether.

True healing does not come from doing more. It comes from becoming more whole.

Mary did not need a bigger title or a smaller one. She needed a definition of a good life that had room in it for her, the person doing the achieving, and not only the achievements. That is what the rest of this chapter is for.

The Success Script You Inherited

Before you can redefine success, it helps to understand where your current definition came from.

Most people did not consciously choose their definition of success. They absorbed it. It arrived through the messages of the environments they were raised in, the culture they came of age in, the institutions that evaluated and rewarded them, and the people whose approval mattered most when they were still forming their sense of who they were and what they were worth.

For many high-achieving individuals, the success script includes some combination of the following beliefs: that achievement is the primary evidence of worth; that busyness signals importance; that financial stability is the ultimate form of security; that recognition from others confirms that effort was real; and that rest, comfort, or satisfaction before reaching a certain level of achievement is premature, even self-indulgent.

These beliefs are not always explicit. They rarely arrive as direct instructions. More often, they are absorbed through observation. You watched who was praised and who was overlooked. You learned what earned approval and what was quietly dismissed. You adapted. Over time, those adaptations became so internalized that you stopped experiencing them as choices.

I know this one from the inside. Growing up, I learned to measure myself by what I could do, because that is where the praise was. I was the good student. I was the one my family was proud of. And when I became a doctor, that became the whole story. People did not introduce me as Tashina. They introduced me as Dr. Tashina, like the title was the point. I am not saying that to complain about it. I am saying it because somewhere in there, I picked up a quiet job I never applied for: keep being the successful one. Keep it together. Perform the version of me that everyone was proud of, even on the days I was nowhere close to having it together. I did not question that script for a long time. It had worked. It had gotten me everything I was supposed to want.

What finally made me question it was simpler than a breakdown. I just got tired. Tired of achieving and still not feeling satisfied, like the finish line moved every time I got near it. It was during the layoff, the one I told you about at the beginning of this book, that I finally sat down and asked what success would look like if it were actually mine.

These days I hold my accomplishments a little differently. My family is proud of me, and I am grateful for that. But I tell people now, you do not have to call me Dr. Tashina. Just call me Tashina. In a professional space, the title is appropriate, and I honor it. Everywhere else, I am just me. Because I am not my titles, and I am more than what I have achieved. I ground myself in who I am, not in the accolades attached to my name. I did not have language for any of this back then. I just knew the chasing never stopped. The research has a name for what I was doing.

Psychologist Carol Dweck, whose research on motivation has been foundational in developmental psychology, distinguishes between performance goals, which focus on demonstrating competence to others, and mastery goals, which focus on developing competence for internal reasons (Dweck, 2006). Much of what gets called ambition in high-achieving adults is more accurately performance orientation, a drive rooted not in genuine desire but in the need to be seen as capable, to avoid being perceived as inadequate, or to maintain a self-image that was built on external validation.

This is not a moral failing. It is a human response to the environments that shaped you. But it is worth naming, because performance orientation is exhausting in a way that mastery orientation is not. When you are driven by the need to prove, no amount of achievement fully resolves the underlying anxiety. The standard simply moves. The bar rises. And you keep running.

Mary had been running a performance race for eighteen years. She had not chosen it deliberately. She had simply followed the script she was handed and executed it extremely well. The problem was never her capability. The problem was that the script had never been hers.

The most important question is not whether you are successful. It is whether your definition of success was ever actually yours.

What the Research Says About Success and Well-Being

There is a meaningful and well-documented gap between the achievements people pursue and the well-being those achievements actually produce.

Psychologists Ed Diener and Martin Seligman, both central figures in the field of positive psychology, have spent decades studying the relationship between external success and subjective well-being. Their research consistently finds that beyond a certain threshold of financial security, additional income has diminishing returns on happiness. More significant predictors of sustained well-being include the quality of relationships, the presence of meaning and purpose, autonomy in daily decisions, and engagement with activities that feel intrinsically rewarding (Diener & Seligman, 2004). These are not factors that traditional success measures capture. And they are precisely the factors that burnout most consistently erodes.

Self-determination theory, which Chapter 11 explored in depth, offers additional clarity on why conventional success can feel hollow even when achieved. Genuine well-being depends on the three core psychological needs of autonomy, competence, and relatedness (Ryan & Deci, 2017), and high-achievement environments frequently satisfy competence while undermining the other two. You become skilled and recognized while slowly losing the sense that your choices are your own and that you are truly known by the people around you.

Research on what psychologists call the hedonic treadmill, a term rooted in the work of Brickman and Campbell, describes the well-documented human tendency to return to a stable baseline level of well-being despite significant positive or negative life changes (Brickman & Campbell, 1971). This means that the promotion, the award, the revenue milestone, all produce a temporary elevation in satisfaction that fades as the new status becomes the new normal. The achievement that was supposed to finally feel like enough simply becomes the new floor from which the next goal is set.

Understanding this is not meant to induce despair. It is meant to free you from a particularly exhausting form of hope, the belief that the next achievement will be the one that finally makes things feel right. It will not. Not because you are broken, but because that is how the human satisfaction system works. Sustainable well-being is not built through accumulation. It is built through alignment.

The False Choice Between Ambition and Peace

One of the most persistent and damaging beliefs in high-achievement culture is that ambition and peace are mutually exclusive. That you must choose between striving and being well. That wanting more and wanting rest are incompatible desires that cannot occupy the same life at the same time.

This is a lie that burnout culture depends on.

Wellness and ambition can coexist.

Let me be clear about something, because I do not want this to be misread. I am still ambitious. My drive is a good thing. It is the engine that moves me toward work I love and purpose I believe in, and I have no interest in shrinking it. What changed is not the ambition. It is the pace, and the reason underneath it. I no longer move like something is chasing me. I am not in competition with anyone but the woman I was yesterday, so what exactly is the rush? I had to unlearn the need to have it done now, and done fast. If something is meant for me, it will be for me. I would rather take my time and arrive whole than sprint there and have nothing left when I do.

That shift did not come easy, and I want to name why. The belief that you have to choose between ambition and peace is not just a personal hang-up. It is protected by something bigger.

It is also, frankly, a convenient one for systems that benefit from your exhaustion. When you believe that peace is a reward for performance rather than a prerequisite for it, you will keep performing at any cost. You will defer your own well-being indefinitely. You will treat yourself as the last item on a list that never gets fully checked off.

The truth, supported by both research and lived experience, is that ambition rooted in genuine values and pursued with sustainable practices produces better outcomes over time than ambition driven by fear, depletion, and the compulsive need to prove. Work on sustainable performance in high-demand fields argues that individuals who maintain practices of recovery, who honor limits rather than chronically overriding them, and who build their professional identity on internal values rather than external validation, tend to demonstrate greater creativity, resilience, and career longevity than those who operate in perpetual overdrive (Loehr & Schwartz, 2003).

Peace does not soften ambition. It grounds it.

What you gain when you stop treating well-being as optional is not a smaller life. It is a more sustainable one. It is the ability to pursue meaningful goals from a place of genuine energy rather than anxiety. It is the capacity to stay engaged over years rather than burning through your reserves in months. It is the experience of actually inhabiting your life rather than sprinting through it toward a finish line that keeps moving. A definition of success that fits your capacity is the only kind you can live inside for the length of an actual life.

Mary eventually understood this distinction not through a revelation but through a small experiment. She began leaving work at a consistent time three days a week, not because there was nothing left to do (there was always something left to do) but because she had decided to test the hypothesis that protecting some of her energy might not destroy her effectiveness. What she found, after several months, was that her best thinking happened in the mornings after those evenings. The distance from the work had not diminished her performance. It had restored the part of her mind that was actually good at the work. Wellness and ambition can coexist. They were never truly at odds. They were only made to seem that way.

New Ways to Measure Success

If the measures you have been using to measure success led you to burnout, they deserve examination.

Traditional success indicators are almost exclusively external and output-based. Revenue generated. Titles held. Followers accumulated. Deals closed. Projects completed. Awards received. These are not meaningless. They can reflect genuine effort, real impact, and hard-won competence. The problem is not that they exist. The problem is when they become the only language available for evaluating a life.

A more complete definition of success includes internal and relational dimensions alongside the external ones. It asks not only what you have accomplished but how you lived while accomplishing it. Not only what you built but who you were in the building of it. Not only what others saw but what was actually true.

Consider what it would mean to measure success by your ability to rest without guilt. By your capacity to be fully present with the people you love. By the alignment between how you spend your time and what you genuinely value. By your emotional well-being at the end of a week rather than only your output. By whether the life you are building is one you would actually want to be living, not just one that looks correct from the outside.

These are not soft measures. They are demanding ones. In some ways, they are harder to meet than revenue targets because they require a level of honest self-knowledge that external achievement allows you to avoid. You can chase a number without knowing yourself. You cannot live in genuine alignment without it.

Values clarification, a process developed within Acceptance and Commitment Therapy by psychologist Steven Hayes, involves identifying the qualities of action and being that matter most to you, independent of external outcomes. Hayes and his colleagues distinguish between goals, which are achievements that can be completed and checked off, and values, which are ongoing orientations that guide how you move through your life regardless of whether any specific outcome is reached (Hayes et al., 2012). A goal is to publish a book. A value is to contribute something honest to the world. The goal can be completed. The value cannot, and does not need to be. It simply informs every decision.

When success is redefined to include values-based living, it becomes both more honest and more durable. It is no longer contingent on a single outcome or a single season. It is something you can participate in daily, in small choices as well as large ones.

Alignment Over Performance

The shift from performance orientation to alignment is not a rejection of achievement. It is a change in the relationship between your achievements and your sense of self.

Performance orientation asks: Am I doing enough to be seen as successful? Alignment asks: Is what I am doing consistent with who I am and what I genuinely value? These questions can produce very similar behaviors on any given day. A person operating from each orientation might work equally hard, pursue equally ambitious goals, and produce equally impressive results. The difference is in what the work costs, what it means, and whether it sustains or depletes the person doing it.

Living in alignment means your decisions are guided by something internal rather than reactive to something external. You choose what fits your values, your capacity, and your genuine vision for your life rather than simply accepting what is available, expected, or most likely to generate approval. You create from purpose rather than from pressure. And when you reach your goals, the satisfaction is real rather than momentary, because the achievement is connected to something that actually matters to you.

This does not mean you will always feel motivated. It does not mean alignment is a permanent state that once found stays fixed. There will be seasons when even work you love feels difficult. There will be days when values-based decisions still produce discomfort. Alignment is not a feeling. It is a practice of continually returning to the question of whether what you are doing reflects who you actually are and what you genuinely care about.

For Mary, alignment began with a conversation she had long avoided, with herself. She sat with a piece of paper and wrote two questions at the top: What do I actually care about? and What am I doing with most of my time? The gap between the two columns was clarifying in a way she had not expected. She cared about mentorship, about her family, about the quality of her thinking, about leaving something behind that reflected her actual values. She was spending most of her time in meetings that generated neither growth nor meaning, managing up in ways that required her to be less honest than she wanted to be, and optimizing for a title she had already earned and no longer needed to prove.

That gap was not a verdict. It was a map. It showed her where the work of redefining success actually needed to happen, not in her performance reviews but in her daily choices about where to put her attention and energy.

You do not have to stop striving. You have to start striving toward something that is actually yours.

Giving Yourself Permission

One of the quietest but most significant barriers to redefining success is permission. Specifically, the permission to want something different from what you have been working toward, to value something that the people around you might not recognize as valuable, and to build a life that looks different from the one that was praised.

Many high-achieving women, in particular, have internalized the message that wanting less external achievement signals insufficiency, while wanting more peace signals weakness. This creates a double bind where you cannot win by your own internal compass because the compass has been calibrated to someone else's north.

Giving yourself permission to redefine success is not the same as settling. It is not giving up or scaling back from fear. It is making a deliberate, honest choice about what you want your life to reflect. It is claiming the authority over your own definition rather than continuing to operate within one you inherited and never consciously agreed to.

Sometimes, redefining success means grieving the version of it you spent years trying to achieve. There is loss in realizing that what you worked so hard for may never have fully fit who you were becoming. That grief is real and worth acknowledging. But on the other side of that grief is something clarifying: the freedom that comes when you stop performing a version of your life and start actually living it.

Redefining success is not giving up. It is finally deciding that your life belongs to you.

I will be honest about how long this took me. There was a season where I was so consumed by what other people might think that it actually got in the way of my own success. I did not want to look like I was showing off. I did not want to be judged. So, I shrank, in little ways, to keep everyone around me comfortable. Somewhere along the way I had absorbed a narrative, part cultural, part personal, that being fully myself was too much. In this season of burnout, I had to look that narrative in the face and trade it for one that actually served me.

Here is what I know now. People are going to have an opinion about you either way, good or bad, and most of the time it has nothing to do with you. Some people simply cannot handle your light or your idiosyncrasies, and that is not yours to manage. So, I stopped dimming it to make others comfortable. My no is my no. My yes is my yes. My maybe is my maybe. And my "I don't know" is just that: I don't know. I am at peace with all of it.

Hard Truth

> Peace is not the reward you get after you build the life.
> It is the thing you build the life out of.

CAPACITY CHECK

Rethink Success

This chapter asked you to examine something that runs deep: the story you have been living about what success means and whether that story is genuinely yours. That is not a question to be answered quickly or lightly. Give yourself real time with what follows.

Reflection Questions

1. Where did your current definition of success come from? Whose voice does it sound like when you imagine what "enough" looks like?
2. What have you achieved that you expected to feel more satisfied by than you did? What does that tell you about the measure you were using?
3. What do you genuinely value that your current definition of success does not account for?
4. What would you pursue differently if you were not trying to prove anything to anyone?
5. What would it mean for your life to feel good, not just look good? What would be present that is not present now?
6. What permission have you been waiting for that you may need to give yourself?

Chapter 13

Building a Life That Supports You: Community, Structure, and Living in Rhythm

"At some point in life the world's beauty becomes enough... It is enough."
~ Toni Morrison

Jasmine had a system for everything except herself. Her client files were immaculate. Her calendar was color-coded down to fifteen-minute blocks. Her household ran with the kind of quiet efficiency that guests admired and she had long since stopped noticing. She had developed workflows, optimized her mornings, automated her billing, and created a family schedule that kept four people moving in the right directions without constant coordination. By any observable measure, Jasmine had her life together.

What she had not built, anywhere in the life she'd set up, was space for her own replenishment.

There was no block on the calendar for rest that was not justified by productivity. No system for protecting the hours before the household woke up from being immediately filled with tasks. No workflow for saying no. No routine that existed solely because it made her feel human rather than functional. She had built her life to operate smoothly, and she had done it so well that it now ran largely on her, quietly and without pause.

The morning Jasmine finally saw this clearly was unremarkable by any external measure. She woke at five-thirty, as she always did, and, before her feet touched the floor, she was already composing the first email of the day in her mind. By the time the coffee finished brewing, she had responded to three messages. By seven she had handled two minor crises, packed lunches, reviewed a contract, and confirmed an afternoon meeting she did not want to attend. At nine she sat down at her desk, opened her laptop, and realized, with a calm that felt almost clinical, that she was already depleted. The day had barely started. She had already given it everything she had.

She did not have a breakdown. She had a recognition. The life she had built was efficient. It was responsible. It functioned. But it had been designed entirely around what others needed from her and almost nothing around what she needed to sustain giving it. She had been maintaining a life that ran on her, not for her.

That distinction became the beginning of everything she changed.

This is the chapter where the internal work of the previous chapters becomes the way your life is actually put together. You have spoken your truth, owned your story, begun uplifting your wellness, started reconnecting with yourself, and begun to redefine what success means to you. All of that is real and necessary. But it lives in a life. And if the life itself, its systems, its structure, its daily rhythms, has not been redesigned to support the person you are becoming, the old patterns will reassert themselves by default.

Willpower is not a sustainable building material. Intention without structure dissolves under pressure. And pressure, in the lives of high-achieving women, is not a temporary condition. It is the terrain.

This chapter is about building the external conditions that make internal transformation sustainable. Not by adding more to your already full life, but by rebuilding how that life is structured so that it gives back as much as it takes.

The Difference Between a Life That Works and a Life That Supports You

These two things can look identical from the outside. They often do.

A life that works is one that meets its obligations. Bills are paid. Deadlines are kept. Relationships are nurtured. Children are fed, clients are served, responsibilities are maintained. It is functional, and it keeps moving forward. From almost any outside vantage point, this kind of life appears successful.

A life that supports you does all of that and also includes the conditions you need to remain well while doing it. It has recovery built into the structure, not as an afterthought or a reward for completion, but as a non-negotiable component of the design. It has margin, the space between what you are asked to give and the outer edge of what you can sustainably offer. It has systems that protect your energy rather than only directing it outward. And it reflects, in its daily rhythm, the values and priorities you have identified as genuinely yours.

When the life you're living doesn't match the life you actually want, that gap is where burnout tends to grow.

Research on occupational stress keeps pointing to two things as the main drivers of burnout: high demands paired with low resources (Demerouti et al., 2001). The Job Demands-Resources model, developed by Arnold Bakker and Evangelia Demerouti, makes the case that burnout does not happen just because your demands are high. It happens because the resources you need to meet them, your time, energy, autonomy, support, and room to recover, run chronically short. So this is not really about personal endurance. It is not that you are not strong enough or disciplined enough. The problem is in how your life is set up, and that is what has to change.

You cannot think your way out of a life that empties you. You have to rebuild it.

The real question is not whether you can handle your life as it stands right now. It is whether your life, as it stands right now, can handle you over the long haul.

Systems: Building a Life That Gives Back

Jasmine did not start with a five-year plan. She started with thirty minutes.

Her first system was embarrassingly simple. She blocked the last thirty minutes of her workday as a non-negotiable transition window: no meetings, no calls, no new messages opened. She used it to close out the day, write three notes about what needed to happen the next morning, and deliberately shift from work mode before walking out of her office. It took three weeks to stop feeling guilty about it. After six weeks, she noticed that she was arriving at the dinner table as a person who was actually present rather than someone still running parallel processes.

That thirty-minute block did not change her workload. It changed the quality of what came after it. And what came after it was her family, her rest, and her own replenishment. Those things deserved a system too.

When most high-achieving people hear the word "systems," they think of productivity. Project management tools. Time-blocking. Efficiency strategies. And while those things have their place, that framing misses something essential.

The systems that matter most in recovery from burnout are not systems for doing more. They are systems for protecting what you need in order to keep doing anything well.

A system, in the most practical sense, is any repeating structure that reduces the amount of active decision-making required to function. Psychologist Roy Baumeister's influential research on ego depletion proposed that willpower and decision-making draw from a limited cognitive resource that becomes depleted with use (Baumeister et al., 1998). More recent research has debated how strong that effect actually is, but the practical observation underneath it has held up: a day full of unmade decisions is experienced as heavier than a day whose recurring decisions were settled in advance. The accumulated weight of micro-decisions throughout a day, what to respond to, what to defer, whether to say yes, how to handle a conflict, is part of what makes high-demand living so draining.

Protective systems reduce that load. They take recurring decisions off the table by making them in advance, while your cognitive resources are intact, so you do not have to remake them daily under pressure.

A boundary you have thought through clearly and communicated in advance is a system. A morning routine that protects the first hour of your day from external demands is a system. A standing rule about what receives your response after a certain hour is a system. A weekly practice of reviewing your commitments against your actual capacity before adding new ones is a system. None of these are complicated. All of them require intentional construction. And once built, they function without requiring you to make the same effortful decision over and over again.

Structure: Creating Stability Without Rigidity

Structure is often misunderstood as constraint. For women who have spent years feeling over-controlled by external demands, the idea of adding more structure to their lives can feel counterintuitive, even threatening. If the problem is that your life already has too many rigid obligations, why would more structure help?

The answer lies in who the structure serves.

The structure that exhausts you is structure imposed by others to serve others' needs. Schedules built around availability to everyone except yourself. Routines defined entirely by external demands. Daily patterns that leave no room for your own replenishment because every hour has already been claimed by something or someone else.

The structure that heals you is structure you design, intentionally, to serve your own needs first. Not exclusively, not selfishly, but first in the order of consideration. Because the research is unambiguous on this point: you cannot consistently offer high-quality presence, care, or performance from a place of chronic depletion. The oxygen-mask principle is not a metaphor. It is neurophysiology.

Research on habit formation shows that once a behavior becomes routine, it no longer requires effortful decision-making to execute. The response happens automatically, triggered by context rather than deliberated in the moment

(Wood & Neal, 2007). This is part of why consistent structure eases the felt experience of a demanding day. When your morning, your transitions, and your recovery follow a familiar rhythm, you are not spending scarce cognitive resources deciding what happens next. The day becomes something you move through with intention rather than something you have to constantly reconstruct.

A few structural elements are worth examining closely.

How you begin your day matters. Many women find that the first forty-five minutes set the tone for everything that follows.

How you transition between major roles or responsibilities matters too. Unmanaged transitions carry the residue of one context into the next.

A reset ritual is the simplest version of this. It is one small, repeatable action that tells your nervous system a role has ended and another is beginning. Jasmine's thirty-minute close was one. It can be far smaller: changing your clothes when you walk in the door, a single slow breath before you open the car, two minutes of silence between the last meeting and the school pickup. The ritual itself does not matter. What matters is that it gives the transition an edge, so one role stops spending your capacity before the next one has even begun.

How you end your workday matters. Without a deliberate close, work simply continues indefinitely, at lower quality.

How you protect time for physical care, movement, nourishment, sleep, matters most of all. These are not self-care luxuries. They are physiological requirements for cognitive and emotional functioning.

And how you build recovery into your week matters. Not at the margins. In the center. As a non-negotiable appointment with your own sustainability.

The goal is not a perfect schedule. The goal is a structure that is resilient enough to hold your well-being even when life is demanding, and flexible enough to adapt without collapsing entirely when circumstances shift.

Structure is not a cage. In the hands of someone recovering from burnout, it is a scaffold. It holds the shape of a life you are rebuilding until that shape becomes natural enough to hold itself.

Sustainability: Designing for the Long Game

There is a version of rebuilding that looks like change but functions like a different form of overextension. You swap the exhausting patterns for new ones that feel intentional and aligned, and then you pursue them with the same relentless intensity that burned you out in the first place. You optimize your morning routine. You read every book on recovery. You turn healing into a performance. And eventually, that too becomes depleting.

It helps to name the shift plainly, because it is the whole difference between the life you are leaving and the one you are building. You have spent a long time in survival, which asks only one question: can I get through today? Sustainability asks a different one: can I keep doing this for years without it costing me myself?

Survival optimizes for today. Sustainability protects the version of you who still has to be here in ten years.

Every structure in this chapter is really an answer to that second question. You are not building a more efficient way to survive. You are building a life you will not need to survive.

Sustainability requires a different relationship with time. It requires thinking not only about what is needed this week or this month, but about what the version of you who is still thriving at fifty, sixty, and beyond actually needs you to protect right now.

Research on long-term performance and career longevity consistently identifies recovery as the variable that distinguishes individuals who sustain high performance over decades from those who peak and burn. Sports science was among the first fields to formalize this understanding. The principle of periodization, originally developed for athletic training, holds that high performance requires deliberate alternation between exertion and recovery, and that attempting to sustain peak output continuously leads not to greater achievement but to degradation of capacity over time (Bompa & Haff, 2009). This principle applies with equal force to cognitive, emotional, and professional performance.

Sustainability also means being honest about your actual capacity rather than your aspirational capacity. There is the person you want to be, who handles everything with grace and operates at full output without rest. And there is the person you actually are, who is human, finite, and doing their genuine best. Sustainable living is designed for the actual person, not the aspirational one.

This requires a particular kind of honesty that high-achieving women often find difficult, because it involves acknowledging limits. In cultures that prize endurance, acknowledging limits can feel like admission of inadequacy. But the research is clear: individuals who accurately assess their own capacity and manage their commitments accordingly are more effective over time, experience less burnout, and maintain higher quality of output than those who chronically overcommit (Maslach & Leiter, 2016). Honesty about capacity is not a weakness. It is a strategy.

Sustainability also means building relationships and environments that can share the load. Many women experiencing burnout have quietly built lives in which they are the one everything and everyone depends on, the person who holds it all together. That setup is both exhausting and fragile. Sustainable systems distribute responsibility. They include other people, other resources, and structures that do not depend entirely on you to hold together.

Jasmine eventually had a conversation with her partner that she had been avoiding for two years. She showed him, literally on paper, what her days looked like and what hers contained that his did not. Not as accusation, but as information. The conversation was difficult. What came out of it was a genuine restructuring of shared responsibility that gave her back four hours each week she had not realized she had lost. Four hours. It was not everything. But it changed the texture of her daily life in ways that rippled outward into her work, her presence, and her sense of herself as someone whose needs mattered in the running of her own home.

Sustainability is not built alone. And it is not built in a single season. It is built over time, through honest conversations, intentional choices, and the gradual accumulation of decisions that honor the long game over the immediate demand.

Community: You Were Not Meant to Rebuild Alone

There is one more structure this chapter has to name, and for a lot of high-achieving women it is the hardest one to actually get to: Community.

It is not that we do not want it. Most of the women I know are wide open to connection. They crave a space full of women who get it. The problem is rarely desire. It is time, and it is trust. When your days are already full, and your capacity is already spent, finding the hours to build real connection feels almost impossible, and finding a genuinely safe space, where you can exhale instead of perform, is harder still. So, connection becomes the thing that keeps getting pushed to next month, and next month never quite comes.

I want to tell you how this shifted for me, because it did not happen the way I expected. As I evolved in business and kept pushing past my own comfort zone, I felt a real disconnect from some of my close friends. They were still my friends; that did not change. But I was growing in a direction they did not always understand, and I needed people around me who did. So, I built new circles. Not to replace anyone, but to add what was missing. I sought out rooms full of like-minded women who understood entrepreneurship, and other rooms for the other parts of me, because we are multidimensional, and no single community can hold all of who we are. That was the shift for me. I stopped expecting one circle to be everything and started letting myself have several. I connected with various professional organizations as a way to keep learning and growing as a businesswoman. Some of those connections became a genuine source of support and respite. And I did it while still protecting my capacity, connecting without overextending, showing up without becoming the one holding everyone together.

There are more kinds of community than we often realize, because community tends to form around shared experience. Right now, in this season of life, there is a community of women moving through perimenopause, menopause, and the years after it, and they are finding each other and making real connections because they are living the same thing at the same time. It might be grief that draws people together. It might be business. It might be something else entirely. Different experiences, different communities, and each one can help balance you out in a different way.

Now, I know naming all of these communities can start to feel like one more demand on your capacity. So let me be clear about what I am not saying. I am not saying join everything under the sun. That would defeat the entire purpose. What I am saying is that meaningful connection with the right community can help you fill your cup, not empty it. The access is there. The work is to first identify what you actually need, then consider your capacity honestly, and then move accordingly. Not more. Just what fills you.

And then there is family, which is its own kind of community. My nephews are my heartbeat. Family and close friends remain an important part of my support system, even as other areas of my life and community have grown. I nurture those relationships in the ways my capacity allows, emotionally, mentally, physically, and sometimes financially. I protect those connections, because they are part of what holds me.

And here is something worth holding onto: your community will shift as you grow, and that is okay. What you need in your forties is not what you needed in your twenties. The woman who is an empty nester now, with her children grown and gone, needs a different kind of community than she did when the house was full. Building community looked different for me at each stage, and it will look different for you too. I will not pretend that is painless. Outgrowing a community, or shifting toward a new one, can be a real loss, and it is okay to grieve it. But outgrowing a season does not erase what it gave you. The relationships that mattered still mattered. They simply look different now, as you evolve and connect in new ways.

Here is what I want you to take from this. The life you are building in these pages is not a solo structure. A circle that shrinks is not a failure. Sometimes it is just making room. But do not confuse making room with doing it alone. Go build the connections that fit who you are becoming. You were never meant to rebuild by yourself.

Living in Rhythm

Rhythm is different from routine. Routine is a fixed sequence of actions. Rhythm is a relationship with time that honors your natural cycles of energy, focus, creativity, and recovery.

Human beings are not built for constant output at uniform intensity. Chronobiology, the scientific study of biological rhythms, has documented extensive evidence for ultradian rhythms, natural cycles of approximately ninety to one hundred and twenty minutes that govern peaks and troughs in cognitive alertness, emotional stability, and physical energy throughout the day (Kleitman, 1982). Most people have been trained to override these rhythms entirely, pushing through natural energy dips with caffeine and urgency rather than honoring them as biological cues for brief recovery. Over time, this chronic override contributes significantly to the accumulated fatigue that burnout represents.

Living in rhythm means learning to recognize your own patterns rather than simply imposing a generic productivity template over them. It means noticing when your thinking is clearest and protecting that time for work that requires real depth. It means recognizing when your energy dips and using those windows for less cognitively demanding tasks, brief movement, or genuine rest rather than fighting through them with diminishing returns. It means honoring the seasonal rhythms of your life, the times of year that are naturally heavier and building more margin into those periods, and the quieter seasons when recovery can be deepened and replenishment can happen at a more generous pace.

Living in rhythm also means releasing the tyranny of uniform productivity. Not every day will look the same. Not every week will produce the same output. The woman who can work at full capacity on Monday should not be expected to match that output on Friday after a depleting week, and building a life that pretends otherwise is a form of self-deception that eventually becomes a form of self-harm.

For Jasmine, living in rhythm began with a deceptively simple practice. At the end of each Sunday evening, she spent fifteen minutes reviewing the coming week, not to optimize it or fill every gap, but to identify where the genuine demands were concentrated and to deliberately protect one period of recovery for every period of high output. She called them her balance points. A harder week at work meant protecting the weekend more intentionally. A significant emotional event meant building in quiet time the following day rather than immediately returning to full pace. She was not always successful. But she was no longer moving through her life entirely reactively, consuming her own reserves without replenishment and wondering why she felt empty.

Rhythm cannot be imposed from the outside. It has to be listened for. It is already in you. The work is not creating it. The work is finally stopping long enough to hear it.

You were not built for constant output. You were built for rhythm. Work and rest. Exertion and recovery. Full presence and quiet restoration. A life that honors that rhythm is not a smaller life. It is a sustainable one.

The Ongoing Work of Building

It is important to end this chapter with honesty about what building a life that supports you actually requires.

It is not a project with a completion date. It is not a set of changes you make once and then maintain effortlessly. Building a supportive life is ongoing work, requiring repeated attention, periodic reassessment, and the willingness to dismantle and rebuild sections that stop working as your circumstances evolve.

There will be seasons when the systems you built stop fitting. A new role, a significant loss, a shift in family needs, a change in your own values and priorities can all require you to return to the drawing board on structures you thought were settled. This is not failure. It is growth. A life that supports you at thirty-five will not look identical to a life that supports you at forty-five.

What you are building here is not a permanent structure. You are building a practice of continual, intentional design. A habit of asking, regularly and honestly, whether the life you are living is structured to support the person you are becoming, or whether it is still running on the old playbook of who you had to be before you understood you had a choice.

Jasmine did not transform her life in a season. She rebuilt it slowly, one system at a time, one conversation at a time, one small protected hour at a time. Two years later, her life still had demands. It still had complexity. It still had hard weeks and seasons when everything felt like too much. But it also had her in it, genuinely in it, present and replenished and capable of giving from a place of genuine abundance rather than chronic scarcity.

That is what you are building toward. Not a life without difficulty. A life in which you remain intact through it.

You have done the internal work. Now build a life that can carry all of who you are, one that protects your capacity instead of quietly spending it.

Hard Truth

Motivation will not keep you well. Systems will.

CAPACITY CHECK

Your Next Steps

This chapter asked you to look honestly at how your daily life is actually set up, not just how it functions on paper, but whether it genuinely supports you. That requires a specific kind of inventory: honest, specific, and without the usual justifications we offer for why things have to be the way they are.

Take your time here. The questions below are designed to surface what may have been invisible: the gaps between the life you have built and the life you need.

Reflection Questions

1. Where in my life am I currently the one everything and everyone depends on, the person holding it all together? What would it take to begin sharing that load?

2. What does my current schedule actually protect, and what does it leave unprotected? What does that reveal about whose needs my life is built around?

Call to Action: Design One Structural Change

Choose one concrete structural change to implement in the next seven days. Not a mindset shift. Not an intention. A specific, observable change to the routine of your daily life.

It should meet three criteria: it should protect something you currently leave unprotected; it should be small enough to actually implement without requiring anyone's permission except your own; and it should reduce, in some measurable way, the gap between the life that currently runs on you and the life that is designed to support you.

Examples might include: a non-negotiable thirty-minute window in your day that belongs entirely to you; a standing "no" to one category of request that consistently drains you without returning value; a conversation with someone in your household or workplace about redistributing a responsibility that is not equitably shared; a weekly fifteen-minute review of your commitments versus your actual capacity before accepting new ones; or a consistent ending time for your workday that is not conditional on everything being finished, because everything is never finished.

Start with one. Build the habit of intentional design. And then, when that structure holds, add another.

A supportive life is not built in a single decision. It is built in the accumulation of decisions made, over time, by someone who has decided that her own sustainability is worth protecting.

That someone is you.

You have done the work to know that now.

Build accordingly.

Conclusion

You Don't Have to Live Like This Anymore

There comes a moment when awareness shifts into something deeper. Not just understanding, not just recognition, but truth. And if you have made it this far, then you already know the truth. You are not just tired. You have been carrying more than your capacity for longer than your body was designed to sustain. You have been performing strength, producing results, holding things together, and pushing forward, even when something in you has been asking you to pause.

This book was never just about burnout. It was about what lives beneath it: the patterns, the pressure, the identity, and the expectations. It was about the parts of you that learned how to survive but never learned how to rest. And now, you know. You see it. You understand it. You have begun to interrupt it. And you have been introduced to a different way of living. One where your well-being is not an afterthought, where your capacity matters, and where you can be both ambitious and well.

Because you can. You can build your life without abandoning yourself. You can pursue more without losing who you are in the process. You can create success that does not cost you your peace.

That version of you is not far away. She is the one who starts choosing differently, not all at once, but moment by moment, boundary by boundary, and decision by decision. This is not about becoming someone new. It is about returning to yourself with awareness, compassion, and intention. And you were never meant to do that alone.

But here is what matters most. At some point, you will be faced with a choice. Not a dramatic, life-altering moment, but a quiet one. A moment where you are asked to keep pushing or to pause. To say yes out of habit or to honor yourself with something different. To perform, or to be present.

And in that moment, everything you have read will meet everything you are ready to live. Because healing is not found in what you know. It is revealed in what you choose.

So when that moment comes, and it will, choose yourself. Not once, not perfectly, but consistently. Choose the version of you who no longer abandons herself to be everything for everyone else. Choose the version of you who understands that peace is not something you earn; it is something you allow. Because you were never meant to survive your life. You were meant to live it. And this is where that life begins.

So, you went beneath it.

That is what this book asked of you, and that is what you did. You went beneath the symptoms and found the patterns. You went beneath the performance and found a person who was never broken, only buried. Burnout was not the whole story. It was the signal that called you back to yourself.

What you found beneath it is yours. It sits in the pause before you answer yes when you mean no. It shows up in the moment you choose your capacity over someone else's expectation. It lives in the rest you finally allow without apology.

Beneath the burnout was not emptiness.

Beneath the burnout was you. And she was worth going down to find.

You are not the same woman you were when you opened Chapter 1.

You have been seen. By these pages, by the women whose stories echoed yours, and by yourself.

An empowered soul has no limits on who she can become. Not because she ignores her capacity, but because she has finally learned to honor it.

Resources

Crisis and Support Resources

You were never meant to carry everything alone, and that includes this book. If anything in these pages stirred something heavy in you, something that feels bigger than a reflection question can hold, please reach out. Asking for support is not a failure of strength. It is one of the most faithful acts of stewardship there is. The resources below are available in the United States; most are free, confidential, and open around the clock.

If You Are in Crisis Right Now

988 Suicide and Crisis Lifeline

Call or text 988, any hour of any day. Online chat is available at 988lifeline.org.

Crisis Text Line

Text HOME to 741741 to connect with a trained crisis counselor, 24/7.

Emergency Services

If you or someone you love is in immediate danger, call 911 or go to the nearest emergency room.

Ongoing Support and Finding Care

SAMHSA National Helpline

1-800-662-4357. Free, confidential, 24/7 treatment referral and information for mental health and substance use concerns.

NAMI HelpLine (National Alliance on Mental Illness)

1-800-950-6264, or text "NAMI" to 62640. Available Monday through Friday, 10:00 a.m. to 10:00 p.m. Eastern. This is a support and information line, not a crisis line. Support, information, and help navigating mental health care.

National Domestic Violence Hotline

1-800-799-7233, or text START to 88788. Confidential support for anyone experiencing abuse, 24/7.

Postpartum Support International

1-800-944-4773. Support for mothers and families navigating perinatal mental health, including the exhaustion and depression this book names.

Therapy for Black Girls

therapyforblackgirls.com. A directory and community for finding culturally competent therapists.

The Loveland Foundation

thelovelandfoundation.org. Therapy funding support for Black women and girls.

Psychology Today Therapist Directory

psychologytoday.com/us/therapists. Search licensed therapists by location, specialty, and insurance.

Phone numbers and websites can change over time. If a resource listed here is no longer active, a search for the organization by name will lead you to its current contact information. And if you are already working with a therapist, a physician, or a trusted counselor, this page is not a replacement for that relationship. It is simply here so that no reader of this book ever has to wonder where to turn.

About the Author

Dr. Tashina Reeder is a licensed social worker, trained clinician, trauma-informed wellness trainer, and founder of Soul Care Services and Soul Care Academy, with over 25 years of clinical experience. She holds a Doctorate in Couple and Family Therapy from Drexel University and a Master of Social Work from Temple University, with advanced training in Prolonged Exposure (PE) Therapy and the Trauma Recovery and Empowerment Model (TREM).

Dr. Reeder specializes in supporting high-achieving women, leaders, and organizations who appear to have everything together on the outside but feel exhausted, disconnected, and overwhelmed on the inside. Her work lives at the intersection of clinical insight and lived experience, helping individuals understand burnout not as a single moment but as a pattern, one built through years of overfunctioning, emotional labor, and unmet capacity. Through her signature work, Beneath the Burnout™, she equips individuals and teams with practical, evidence-based, and culturally responsive tools to restore balance, strengthen emotional regulation, and lead with clarity and intention.

A nationally and internationally recognized speaker and trainer, Dr. Reeder has shared her message of wellness and sustainable success across Trinidad, St. Thomas, the Bahamas, Ghana, and her home base of Philadelphia. Her work bridges the gap between mental health, leadership, and lived experience, making complex concepts accessible and actionable. Her impact has been recognized with honors including the Presidential Lifetime Achievement Award, the Strength in Healing Wellness Award, and the Women Who Lead Community Impact Award.

Dr. Reeder's work is grounded in the belief that wellness and ambition can coexist, and that soul care is not indulgent, it is foundational. When individuals prioritize it, they unlock their capacity to heal, grow, reconnect with themselves, and build lives that are both meaningful and sustainable.

Her motto: An Empowered Soul Has No Limits.

Your Next Step Starts Here

Finishing this book is not the end of your healing; it is the beginning of living differently.

If you're ready to move beyond awareness and begin creating lasting change, I'd love to continue the journey with you. Whether you're looking for coaching, professional training, a keynote speaker, workshops, or wellness resources, there are several ways we can work together to support your personal or professional goals.

Not sure where to begin?

Schedule a consultation to explore your needs and determine which service, program, or resource is the best fit for you.

Learn more:

www.soulcareservices.org (or scan the QR code below)

SCAN ME

Join the Community

You don't have to do this work alone.

Join Soulfully Her, my private Facebook community for women committed to protecting their peace, honoring their capacity, and choosing wellness one intentional step at a time.

Scan the QR code below to join.

SCAN ME

References

Abrams, J. A., Hill, A., & Maxwell, M. (2019). Underneath the mask of the strong Black woman schema: Disentangling influences of strength and self-silencing on depressive symptoms among U.S. Black women. *Sex Roles, 80*(9–10), 517–526. https://doi.org/10.1007/s11199-018-0956-y

Ali, O. M., Milstein, G., & Marzuk, P. M. (2005). The imam's role in meeting the counseling needs of Muslim communities in the United States. *Psychiatric Services, 56*(2), 202–205. https://doi.org/10.1176/appi.ps.56.2.202

American Psychological Association. (2023). *Stress in America™ 2023: A nation recovering from collective trauma*. https://www.apa.org

Arnsten, A. F. T. (2009). Stress signalling pathways that impair prefrontal cortex structure and function. *Nature Reviews Neuroscience, 10*(6), 410–422. https://doi.org/10.1038/nrn2648

Assor, A., & Tal, K. (2012). When parents' affection depends on child's achievement: Parental conditional positive regard, self-aggrandizement, shame and coping in adolescents. *Journal of Adolescence, 35*(2), 249–260. https://doi.org/10.1016/j.adolescence.2011.10.004

Barna Group. (2022, April 27). *Pastors share top reasons they've considered quitting ministry in the past year*. https://www.barna.com/research/pastors-quitting-ministry/

Barrett, L. F. (2017). *How emotions are made: The secret life of the brain*. Houghton Mifflin Harcourt.

Baumeister, R. F., Bratslavsky, E., Muraven, M., & Tice, D. M. (1998). Ego depletion: Is the active self a limited resource? *Journal of Personality and Social Psychology, 74*(5), 1252–1265. https://doi.org/10.1037/0022-3514.74.5.1252

Bellezza, S., Paharia, N., & Keinan, A. (2017). Conspicuous consumption of time: When busyness and lack of leisure time become a status symbol. *Journal of Consumer Research, 44*(1), 118–138. https://doi.org/10.1093/jcr/ucw076

Bloom, M. (2019). *Flourishing in ministry: How to cultivate clergy wellbeing.* Rowman & Littlefield.

Bloom, S. L. (2017). The Sanctuary Model: Through the lens of moral safety. In J. Cook, C. J. Dalenberg, & S. N. Gold (Eds.), *APA handbook of trauma psychology: Vol. 2. Trauma practice* (pp. 469–490). American Psychological Association.

Bloom, S. L., McKinney, J., Valdes, A., Tracy, C., & DeRiggi, L. (2007). *Provider requirements and staff competencies in a trauma-informed system of care*. Philadelphia Department of Behavioral Health.

Bompa, T. O., & Haff, G. G. (2009). *Periodization: Theory and methodology of training* (5th ed.). Human Kinetics.

Brickman, P., & Campbell, D. T. (1971). Hedonic relativism and planning the good society. In M. H. Appley (Ed.), *Adaptation-level theory* (pp. 287–302). Academic Press.

Bride, B. E. (2007). Prevalence of secondary traumatic stress among social workers. *Social Work, 52*(1), 63–70. https://doi.org/10.1093/sw/52.1.63

Brown, B. (2012). *Daring greatly: How the courage to be vulnerable transforms the way we live, love, parent, and lead*. Gotham Books.

Chisolm, A. (2024, December 16). *How the 92 percent of Black women are interpreting the election results*. Black Girl Nerds. https://blackgirlnerds.com/how-the-92-percent-of-black-women-are-interpreting-the-election-results/

Church of God in Christ. (2024, February 29). *COGIC launches first national mental health PSA's*. https://www.cogic.org/blog/cogic-launches-first-national-mental-health-psas/

Crocker, J., & Park, L. E. (2004). The costly pursuit of self-esteem. *Psychological Bulletin, 130*(3), 392–414. https://doi.org/10.1037/0033-2909.130.3.392

Dalton-Smith, S. (2017). *Sacred rest: Recover your life, renew your energy, restore your sanity*. FaithWords.

Deci, E. L., & Ryan, R. M. (2000). The "what" and "why" of goal pursuits: Human needs and the self-determination of behavior. *Psychological Inquiry, 11*(4), 227–268. https://doi.org/10.1207/S15327965PLI1104_01

Demerouti, E., Bakker, A. B., Nachreiner, F., & Schaufeli, W. B. (2001). The job demands–resources model of burnout. *Journal of Applied Psychology, 86*(3), 499–512. https://doi.org/10.1037/0021-9010.86.3.499

Dempsey, K. (2002). Who gets the best deal from marriage: Women or men? *Journal of Sociology, 38*(2), 91–110. https://doi.org/10.1177/144078302128756525

Diener, E., & Seligman, M. E. P. (2004). Beyond money: Toward an economy of well-being. *Psychological Science in the Public Interest, 5*(1), 1–31. https://doi.org/10.1111/j.0963-7214.2004.00501001.x

Duke Clergy Health Initiative. (n.d.). *Clergy Health Initiative*. Duke Divinity School. https://divinity.duke.edu/initiatives/clergy-health-initiative

Dweck, C. S. (2006). *Mindset: The new psychology of success*. Random House.

Edmondson, A. C. (1999). Psychological safety and learning behavior in work teams. *Administrative Science Quarterly, 44*(2), 350–383. https://doi.org/10.2307/2666999

Fredrickson, B. L. (2001). The role of positive emotions in positive psychology: The broaden-and-build theory of positive emotions. *American Psychologist, 56*(3), 218–226. https://doi.org/10.1037/0003-066X.56.3.218

Freeman, M. A., Staudenmaier, P. J., Zisser, M. R., & Andresen, L. A. (2019). The prevalence and co-occurrence of psychiatric conditions among entrepreneurs and their families. *Small Business Economics, 53*(2), 323–342. https://doi.org/10.1007/s11187-018-0059-8

Gallup, Inc. (2015). *State of the American manager: Analytics and advice for leaders*. Gallup Press.

Gavelin, H. M., Domellöf, M. E., Åström, E., Nelson, A., Launder, N. H., Neely, A. S., & Lampit, A. (2022). Cognitive function in clinical burnout: A systematic review and meta-analysis. *Work & Stress, 36*(1), 86–104. https://doi.org/10.1080/02678373.2021.2002972

Gaylor, E. M., Krause, K. H., Welder, L. E., Cooper, A. C., Ashley, C., Mack, K. A., Crosby, A. E., Trinh, E., Ivey-Stephenson, A. Z., & Whittle, L. (2023). Suicidal thoughts and behaviors among high school students — Youth Risk Behavior Survey, United States, 2021. *MMWR Supplements, 72*(1), 45–54. https://doi.org/10.15585/mmwr.su7201a6

Geronimus, A. T. (1992). The weathering hypothesis and the health of African American women and infants. *Ethnicity & Disease, 2*(3), 207–221.

Geronimus, A. T., Hicken, M., Keene, D., & Bound, J. (2006). "Weathering" and age patterns of allostatic load scores among Blacks and Whites in the United States. *American Journal of Public Health, 96*(5), 826–833. https://doi.org/10.2105/AJPH.2004.060749

Gross, J. J. (1998). Antecedent- and response-focused emotion regulation: Divergent consequences for experience, expression, and physiology. *Journal of Personality and Social Psychology, 74*(1), 224–237. https://doi.org/10.1037/0022-3514.74.1.224

Gross, J. J., & Levenson, R. W. (1997). Hiding feelings: The acute effects of inhibiting positive and negative emotion. *Journal of Abnormal Psychology, 106*(1), 95–103. https://doi.org/10.1037/0021-843X.106.1.95

Hayes, S. C., Strosahl, K. D., & Wilson, K. G. (2012). *Acceptance and commitment therapy: The process and practice of mindful change* (2nd ed.). Guilford Press.

Helfrich, C. D., Simonetti, J. A., Clinton, W. L., Wood, G. B., Taylor, L., Schectman, G., Stark, R., Rubenstein, L. V., Fihn, S. D., & Nelson, K. M. (2017). The association of team-specific workload and staffing with odds of burnout among VA primary care team members. *Journal of General Internal Medicine, 32*(7), 760–766. https://doi.org/10.1007/s11606-017-4011-4

Hochschild, A. R. (1983). *The managed heart: Commercialization of human feeling*. University of California Press.

Hochschild, A. R., & Machung, A. (2012). *The second shift: Working families and the revolution at home* (Updated ed.). Penguin Books.

Impett, E. A., Gable, S. L., & Peplau, L. A. (2005). Giving up and giving in: The costs and benefits of daily sacrifice in intimate relationships. *Journal of Personality and Social Psychology, 89*(3), 327–344. https://doi.org/10.1037/0022-3514.89.3.327

Kahn, R. L., Wolfe, D. M., Quinn, R. P., Snoek, J. D., & Rosenthal, R. A. (1964). *Organizational stress: Studies in role conflict and ambiguity*. John Wiley & Sons.

Kleitman, N. (1982). Basic rest-activity cycle: 22 years later. *Sleep, 5*(4), 311–317. https://doi.org/10.1093/sleep/5.4.311

LeanIn.Org & McKinsey & Company. (2022). *Women in the workplace 2022*. https://leanin.org/women-in-the-workplace/2022

LePera, N. (2021). *How to do the work: Recognize your patterns, heal from your past, and create your self*. Harper Wave.

Leung, D. Y. P., Chan, H. Y. L., Chiu, P. K. C., Lo, R. S. K., & Lee, L. L. Y. (2020). Source of social support and caregiving self-efficacy on caregiver burden and patient's quality of life: A path analysis on patients with palliative care needs and their caregivers. *International Journal of Environmental Research and Public Health, 17*(15), Article 5457. https://doi.org/10.3390/ijerph17155457

Loehr, J., & Schwartz, T. (2003). *The power of full engagement: Managing energy, not time, is the key to high performance and personal renewal*. Free Press.

Marken, S., & Agrawal, S. (2022, June 13). *K-12 workers have highest burnout rate in U.S.* Gallup. https://news.gallup.com/poll/393500/workers-highest-burnout-rate.aspx

Maslach, C., & Leiter, M. P. (2016). Understanding the burnout experience: Recent research and its implications. *World Psychiatry, 15*(2), 103–111. https://doi.org/10.1002/wps.20311

Maslach, C., & Leiter, M. P. (2022). *The burnout challenge: Managing people's relationships with their jobs*. Harvard University Press.

McEwen, B. S. (2007). Physiology and neurobiology of stress and adaptation: Central role of the brain. *Physiological Reviews, 87*(3), 873–904. https://doi.org/10.1152/physrev.00041.2006

Mikhail, A. (2024, May 2). Loneliness at work gets worse for women as they advance. *Fortune*. https://fortune.com/2024/05/02/loneliness-at-work-women-executives-research/

Mikolajczak, M., Brianda, M. E., Avalosse, H., & Roskam, I. (2018). Consequences of parental burnout: Its specific effect on child neglect and violence. *Child Abuse & Neglect, 80*, 134–145. https://doi.org/10.1016/j.chiabu.2018.03.025

Mikolajczak, M., & Roskam, I. (2018). A theoretical and clinical framework for parental burnout: The balance between risks and resources (BR^2). *Frontiers in Psychology, 9*, 886. https://doi.org/10.3389/fpsyg.2018.00886

Neff, K. (2011). *Self-compassion: The proven power of being kind to yourself.* William Morrow.

Newell, J. M., & MacNeil, G. A. (2010). Professional burnout, vicarious traumatization, secondary traumatic stress, and compassion fatigue: A review of theoretical terms, risk factors, and preventive methods for clinicians and researchers. *Best Practices in Mental Health, 6*(2), 57–68.

Obama, M., & Robinson, C. (Hosts). (2025, April 23). You need to learn to say no (even to an inauguration) with Taraji P. Henson [Audio podcast episode]. In *IMO with Michelle Obama & Craig Robinson*. Higher Ground. https://www.imopod.com/episodes/you-need-to-learn-to-say-no-even-to-an-inauguration-with-taraji-p-henson

Pearlin, L. I., Mullan, J. T., Semple, S. J., & Skaff, M. M. (1990). Caregiving and the stress process: An overview of concepts and their measures. *The Gerontologist, 30*(5), 583–594. https://doi.org/10.1093/geront/30.5.583

Pinquart, M., & Sörensen, S. (2003). Differences between caregivers and noncaregivers in psychological health and physical health: A meta-analysis. *Psychology and Aging, 18*(2), 250–267. https://doi.org/10.1037/0882-7974.18.2.250

Porges, S. W. (2011). *The polyvagal theory: Neurophysiological foundations of emotions, attachment, communication, and self-regulation*. W. W. Norton & Company.

Rizzo, K. M., Schiffrin, H. H., & Liss, M. (2013). Insight into the parenthood paradox: Mental health outcomes of intensive mothering. *Journal of Child and Family Studies, 22*(5), 614–620. https://doi.org/10.1007/s10826-012-9615-z

Roepke, S. K., Mausbach, B. T., Patterson, T. L., Depp, C. A., Marino, P., Mills, P. J., Ancoli-Israel, S., Ziegler, M. G., Dimsdale, J. E., & Grant, I. (2011). Effects of Alzheimer caregiving on allostatic load. *Journal of Health Psychology, 16*(1), 58–69. https://doi.org/10.1177/1359105310369188

Roskam, I., & Mikolajczak, M. (2020). Gender differences in the nature, antecedents and consequences of parental burnout. *Sex Roles, 83*(7–8), 485–498. https://doi.org/10.1007/s11199-020-01121-4

Roskam, I., Aguiar, J., Akgun, E., Arikan, G., Artavia, M., Avalosse, H., . . . Mikolajczak, M. (2021). Parental burnout around the globe: A 42-country study. *Affective Science, 2*(1), 58–79. https://doi.org/10.1007/s42761-020-00028-4

Ryan, R. M., & Deci, E. L. (2017). *Self-determination theory: Basic psychological needs in motivation, development, and wellness*. Guilford Press.

Sapolsky, R. M. (2004). *Why zebras don't get ulcers* (3rd ed.). Henry Holt and Company.

Saxbe, D. E., & Repetti, R. (2010). No place like home: Home tours correlate with daily patterns of mood and cortisol. *Personality and Social Psychology Bulletin, 36*(1), 71–81. https://doi.org/10.1177/0146167209352864

Schonfeld, I. S., & Bianchi, R. (2016). *Burnout and depression: Two entities or one? Journal of Clinical Psychology, 72*(1), 22–37. https://doi.org/10.1002/jclp.22229

Schulz, R., & Beach, S. R. (1999). Caregiving as a risk factor for mortality: The Caregiver Health Effects Study. *JAMA, 282*(23), 2215–2219. https://doi.org/10.1001/jama.282.23.2215

Shanafelt, T. D., West, C. P., Dyrbye, L. N., Trockel, M., Tutty, M., Wang, H., Carlasare, L. E., & Sinsky, C. (2022). Changes in burnout and satisfaction with work-life integration in physicians during the first 2 years of the COVID-19 pandemic. *Mayo Clinic Proceedings, 97*(12), 2248–2258. https://doi.org/10.1016/j.mayocp.2022.09.002

Skaalvik, E. M., & Skaalvik, S. (2017). Dimensions of teacher burnout: Relations with potential stressors at school. *Social Psychology of Education, 20*(4), 775–790. https://doi.org/10.1007/s11218-017-9391-0

Smith, M. M., Vidovic, V., Sherry, S. B., Stewart, S. H., & Saklofske, D. H. (2018). Are perfectionism dimensions risk factors for anxiety symptoms? A meta-analysis of 11 longitudinal studies. *Anxiety, Stress, & Coping, 31*(1), 4–20. https://doi.org/10.1080/10615806.2017.1384466

Sonnentag, S., & Bayer, U.-V. (2005). Switching off mentally: Predictors and consequences of psychological detachment from work during off-job time. *Journal of Occupational Health Psychology, 10*(4), 393–414. https://doi.org/10.1037/1076-8998.10.4.393

Sonnentag, S., & Fritz, C. (2015). Recovery from job stress: The stressor-detachment model as an integrative framework. *Journal of Organizational Behavior, 36*(S1), S72–S103. https://doi.org/10.1002/job.1924

Steiner, E. D., Doan, S., Woo, A., Gittens, A. D., Lawrence, R. A., Berdie, L., Wolfe, R. L., Greer, L., & Schwartz, H. L. (2022). *Restoring teacher and principal well-being is an essential step for rebuilding schools: Findings from the State of the American Teacher and State of the American Principal surveys* (RR-A1108-4). RAND Corporation. https://www.rand.org/pubs/research_reports/RRA1108-4.html

Substance Abuse and Mental Health Services Administration. (2014). *SAMHSA's concept of trauma and guidance for a trauma-informed approach* (HHS Publication No. SMA 14-4884). U.S. Department of Health and Human Services.

Suicide Prevention Resource Center. (2025). *Soul Shop for Black Churches* [Best Practices Registry listing]. https://sprc.org/

Sull, D., Sull, C., & Zweig, B. (2022). Toxic culture is driving the Great Resignation. *MIT Sloan Management Review, 63*(2). https://sloanreview.mit.edu/article/toxic-culture-is-driving-the-great-resignation/

Tavella, G., Hadzi-Pavlovic, D., & Parker, G. (2021). Burnout: Redefining its key symptoms. *Psychiatry Research, 302*, Article 114023. https://doi.org/10.1016/j.psychres.2021.114023

van der Kolk, B. (2014). *The body keeps the score: Brain, mind, and body in the healing of trauma*. Viking.

Walker, P. (2013). *Complex PTSD: From surviving to thriving: A guide and map for recovering from childhood trauma*. Azure Coyote Publishing.

Weeks, A. C., & Ruppanner, L. (2025). A typology of US parents' mental loads: Core and episodic cognitive labor. *Journal of Marriage and Family, 87*(3), 966–989. https://doi.org/10.1111/jomf.13057

Williams, L., Gorman, R., & Hankerson, S. (2014). Implementing a mental health ministry committee in faith-based organizations: The promoting emotional wellness and spirituality program. *Social Work in Health Care, 53*(4), 414–434. https://doi.org/10.1080/00981389.2014.880391

Wood, W., & Neal, D. T. (2007). A new look at habits and the habit–goal interface. *Psychological Review, 114*(4), 843–863. https://doi.org/10.1037/0033-295X.114.4.843

Woods-Giscombé, C. L. (2010). Superwoman schema: African American women's views on stress, strength, and health. *Qualitative Health Research, 20*(5), 668–683. https://doi.org/10.1177/1049732310361892

World Health Organization. (2019). *Burn-out an "occupational phenomenon": International Classification of Diseases (11th revision).* https://www.who.int

Wurm, W., Vogel, K., Holl, A., Ebner, C., Bayer, D., Mörkl, S., Szilagyi, I.-S., Hotter, E., Kapfhammer, H.-P., & Hofmann, P. (2016). Depression-burnout overlap in physicians. *PLoS ONE, 11*(3), Article e0149913. https://doi.org/10.1371/journal.pone.0149913

Yanosy, S. M., Harrison, L. C., & Bloom, S. L. (2015). *Sanctuary Model community implementation guide* (Edition 1). ANDRUS Sanctuary Institute.

Zadow, A. J., Dollard, M. F., Dormann, C., & Landsbergis, P. (2021). Predicting new major depression symptoms from long working hours, psychosocial safety climate and work engagement: A population-based cohort study. *BMJ Open, 11*(6), Article e044133. https://doi.org/10.1136/bmjopen-2020-044133